SECOND EDITION

OpenShift for Developers
A Guide for Impatient Beginners

Joshua Wood and Brian Tannous

Beijing · Boston · Farnham · Sebastopol · Tokyo

OpenShift for Developers

by Joshua Wood and Brian Tannous

Copyright © 2021 O'Reilly Media. All rights reserved.

Published by O'Reilly Media, Inc., 1005 Gravenstein Highway North, Sebastopol, CA 95472.

O'Reilly books may be purchased for educational, business, or sales promotional use. Online editions are also available for most titles (*http://oreilly.com*). For more information, contact our corporate/institutional sales department: 800-998-9938 or *corporate@oreilly.com*.

Acquisitions Editor: Suzanne McQuade
Development Editor: Nicole Taché
Production Editor: Katherine Tozer
Copyeditor: Audrey Doyle
Proofreader: Piper Editorial Consulting, LLC

Indexer: Potomac Indexing, LLC
Interior Designer: David Futato
Cover Designer: Karen Montgomery
Illustrator: Kate Dullea

September 2021: Second Edition

Revision History for the Second Edition
2021-09-02: First Release

See *http://oreilly.com/catalog/errata.csp?isbn=9781098103361* for release details.

978-1-098-10336-1

[LSI]

To Randy Wood

–Joshua

To Skeeter

–Brian

Table of Contents

Preface

Software serves more people more critically than ever before. These two demands are generalized as scale and reliability. Over the past decade, the software industry has pursued scale and reliability with tactics, infrastructure, and cultural initiatives like DevOps, which sees developers share the operational responsibility of keeping applications running.

One set of tactics is the automation of operations chores: writing software to run your software. The automation of repetitive toil is among the keystones of Site Reliability Engineering (SRE), an IT discipline defined by the O'Reilly title of the same name. DevOps and its younger cousin GitOps both apply SRE's automation ideas to development machinery and to the practice of building software. The simplest form might be the triggering of automatic construction and deployment processes whenever an application's source code changes.

Modern software infrastructure pursues scale and reliability through *distributed computing*. Despite all the syllables, distributed computing just means making many computers act like one big computer. The assembled system can do more work (scale), and it can cast understudies for potential points of failure (reliability).

Kubernetes is a system for managing applications on distributed computers by encapsulating them in discrete, interchangeable artifacts called *containers*. Kubernetes can manage where and when containers run without knowing all about them and their dependencies. Kubernetes is termed a *container orchestrator*.

OpenShift uses Kubernetes orchestration at its core to harness computers together into a *cluster*. The computers that form the cluster are called *nodes*. OpenShift defines how those nodes relate and how work is performed on them. By packaging core distributed computing primitives with tools, policies, and interfaces for using them, OpenShift helps teams adopt modern practices from DevOps and GitOps and automate repetitive processes according to SRE precepts.

Who This Book Is For

If you're an application developer familiar with data structures and functions and how to build them into programs, but you're new to containers, Kubernetes, and application platforms, this guide to OpenShift is for you. It will show you how to use OpenShift to build, deploy, scale, and manage your software, and how you can automate those chores with OpenShift features such as build triggers, pipelines, and demand-driven autoscaling. You don't need to have used Kubernetes or OpenShift before.

What You Will Learn

This book explains what OpenShift is and how to use it to build your applications, run them, and keep them running through changing demand, failure recovery, and a continuous stream of new releases as you iterate on their source code with new fixes and features.

- Chapters 1 and 2 introduce OpenShift, its components, and its concepts.

- Chapter 3 shows you how to run OpenShift on your computer so that you have a virtual cluster to conduct the book's exercises.

- In Chapter 4, you'll configure OpenShift to fetch the source code for a simple Hello World application, build it into a container image, and run it.

- Chapter 5 introduces OpenShift Pipelines, a framework for composing Continuous Integration and Continuous Deployment (CI/CD) routines, and shows you how to add Pipelines to your cluster.

- In Chapter 6, you'll deploy a more realistic application with a tiered architecture and multiple components.

- In Chapter 7, you'll augment the application's backend to retain data between sessions.

- Chapter 8 shows you how to examine, manipulate, and scale the running application both manually and automatically, how to set up OpenShift to periodically check application health, and how to govern the rollout of new versions of your application.

- Chapter 9 is a high-level overview of OpenShift's monitoring and alerting facilities.

- Chapter 10 dissects OpenShift automation features you used along the way to set you on the path toward eliminating toil by letting the platform do the repetitive work.

Conventions Used in This Book

The following typographical conventions are used in this book:

Italic
> Indicates new terms, URLs, email addresses, filenames, and file extensions.

`Constant width`
> Used for program listings, as well as within paragraphs to refer to program elements such as variable or function names, databases, data types, environment variables, statements, and keywords.

Bold
> Shows commands or other text that should be typed literally by the user.

This element signifies a tip or suggestion.

This element signifies a general note.

This element indicates a warning or caution.

Using Code Examples

Supplemental material (code examples, exercises, etc.) is available for download at *https://github.com/openshift-for-developers*.

If you have a technical question or a problem using the code examples, please send email to *bookquestions@oreilly.com*.

This book is here to help you get your job done. In general, if example code is offered with this book, you may use it in your programs and documentation. You do not need to contact us for permission unless you're reproducing a significant portion of the code. For example, writing a program that uses several chunks of code from this book does not require permission. Selling or distributing examples from O'Reilly books does require permission. Answering a question by citing this book and quoting example code does not require permission. Incorporating a significant amount of example code from this book into your product's documentation does require permission.

We appreciate, but generally do not require, attribution. An attribution usually includes the title, author, publisher, and ISBN. For example: "*OpenShift for Developers*, 2nd edition by Joshua Wood and Brian Tannous (O'Reilly). Copyright 2021 O'Reilly Media, 978-1-098-10336-1."

If you feel your use of code examples falls outside fair use or the permission given here, feel free to contact us at *permissions@oreilly.com*.

O'Reilly Online Learning

 For more than 40 years, *O'Reilly Media* has provided technology and business training, knowledge, and insight to help companies succeed.

Our unique network of experts and innovators share their knowledge and expertise through books, articles, and our online learning platform. O'Reilly's online learning platform gives you on-demand access to live training courses, in-depth learning paths, interactive coding environments, and a vast collection of text and video from O'Reilly and 200+ other publishers. For more information, visit *http://oreilly.com*.

How to Contact Us

Please address comments and questions concerning this book to the publisher:

O'Reilly Media, Inc.
1005 Gravenstein Highway North
Sebastopol, CA 95472
800-998-9938 (in the United States or Canada)
707-829-0515 (international or local)
707-829-0104 (fax)

We have a web page for this book, where we list errata, examples, and any additional information. You can access this page at *https://oreil.ly/openshift-for-developers-2*.

Email *bookquestions@oreilly.com* to comment or ask technical questions about this book.

For news and information about our books and courses, visit *http://oreilly.com*.

Find us on Facebook: *http://facebook.com/oreilly*

Follow us on Twitter: *http://twitter.com/oreillymedia*

Watch us on YouTube: *http://www.youtube.com/oreillymedia*

Acknowledgments

We'd like to thank the Red Hat OpenShift team, and especially the OpenShift Developer Advocates group, specifically for their support as we created this text and generally for their endless efforts to refine and augment OpenShift since its initial release in 2011. As OpenShift grew from pioneer platform to later adopt a Kubernetes core, its goal has remained the same: automate and streamline the work of running applications on modern, massively scalable infrastructure to let developers focus on their code. This book shares that goal.

We also thank those who edited, fact-checked, suggested, occasionally ridiculed, and in so many ways lent their time and minds to make this book more useful and consistent, among them Jason Dobies, Daniel Hinojosa, and Tero Ahonen. Sun Seng David Tan (*https://github.com/sunix*) created the original code on which we based the book's main example application, "Noted," and our families and friends tolerated us while we wrote it.

CHAPTER 1

A Kubernetes Application Platform

OpenShift gives your applications distributed computing power without forcing you to become a distributed computing expert. Translated into jargon, that means Open-Shift is a platform as a service (PaaS).

OpenShift includes tools for building applications from source in composable pipelines. It adds a browser-based graphical interface, the OpenShift Web Console, for deploying and managing workloads. You can point and click to set up network connections, monitoring and alerts, and rules for automatically scaling workloads. An OpenShift cluster applies software updates to itself and its nodes without cluster downtime.

OpenShift is a product from Red Hat. You can run it on your laptop, on a cluster of physical or virtual machines, on all the major cloud providers, and as a managed service. Like most software from Red Hat, OpenShift is developed as an open source project, the OpenShift Kubernetes Distribution (OKD) (*https://www.okd.io*). Open-Shift is in turn built atop two open source keystones: application containers and the Kubernetes container orchestrator.

Linux Containers

Containers are an atomic unit of execution. Each running instance of a container is stamped from an Open Container Initiative (OCI) image (*https://oreil.ly/ZjwqR*) that packages an application executable with all the pieces it needs to run. These dependencies can include shared libraries, auxiliary programs, language runtimes, and anything else the application requires. Such a self-contained parcel is easier to distribute among a team, in a continuous series of releases on a server, and to arbitrary nodes in a cluster.

Container images are stored in a repository often called a *container registry*. Linux kernel facilities isolate and mediate running containers. A running container has its own filesystem and a defined share of the resources of the node where it runs. This isolation allows an orchestrator to schedule containers on a node with sufficient resources without evaluating every other workload running there for potential conflicts in filenames, network port numbers, or other resources.

Kubernetes

OpenShift is a distribution of Kubernetes. Kubernetes is an open source project started at Google and developed by a group of companies and individuals since its release in 2014. This community has adopted formal governance through the Cloud Native Computing Foundation (CNCF) (*https://cncf.io*). Red Hat has been a leading contributor to Kubernetes since the project began, and OpenShift is developed in collaboration with the Kubernetes community.

Kubernetes in OpenShift is like the Linux kernel in a Linux distribution. A Linux distribution combines the kernel with the more familiar programs you use directly. It also makes some basic choices about how you log in, where your files are stored, and what software is essential, letting you do useful work with the system without building it entirely from scratch.

Kubernetes defines a set of common resources and an API for manipulating them. Those resources describe the desired state and track the actual state of the cluster and the things running on it. Kubernetes tries to make the actual state of a resource match its desired state. It repeats this for the life of the cluster. This continuous cycle of watching and tending is called the *reconcile loop*.

Kubernetes alone isn't enough to sustain software in production. There are many decisions to make and components to configure before you can do much with it. Imagine you have the source code for an application and the job of deploying it on a Kubernetes cluster. How will you compile the source code or pair it with its interpreter for packaging in a container image? Will your build process need other computing resources, such as a specialized build server? Once the image is constructed, where will it be stored so that your cluster can access it? A public container registry (and external dependency) like Docker Hub (*https://hub.docker.com*) or Quay (*https://quay.io*)? Or will you need to run your own registry? Your program likely depends on other programs, like a database or application server. Where and how will those run? Can you run them on the cluster, or will you have to maintain another system? These are basic considerations. Addressing them yields a running pod and a new set of questions: How should your application connect with the outside world? How should the power to scale the application, or deploy new versions of it, be governed?

What OpenShift Adds

OpenShift builds atop its Kubernetes core to add features and the components that support them. Some of its original developers called Kubernetes "a platform for building platforms." OpenShift took them up on it. It provides the automation and resilience of modern infrastructure while letting you stay focused on your application code (Figure 1-1).

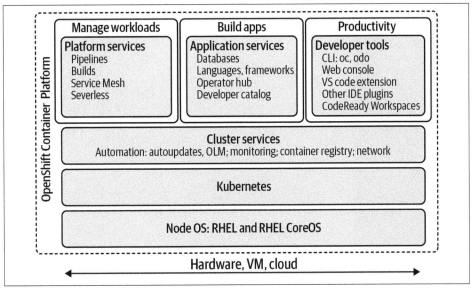

Figure 1-1. OpenShift around a Kubernetes core

This book focuses on the features you'll use to run your applications. It is not an OpenShift system administration guide. The next section previews some of Open-Shift's developer features. You'll use most of them in the following chapters.

Web Console

The OpenShift Web Console is a graphical view of the cluster and your applications. As the name suggests, it runs in a web browser. The Web Console lets you do everything necessary to deploy and run your software projects with graphical controls and forms for configuration, rather than sifting through so many lines and indentations of underlying YAML. The console depicts connections between services with a topological view of application components, and shows project, application, and container resource consumption with graphical gauges and charts (Figure 1-2).

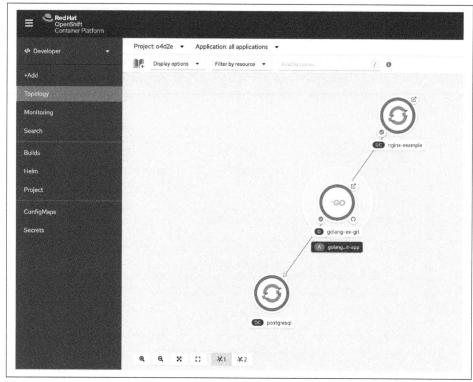

Figure 1-2. OpenShift Web Console showing the topology of an application's components

Curated Software Catalogs: An OpenShift App Store

The Web Console also aggregates software catalogs, from application templates to Kubernetes Operators. The OperatorHub inside the Web Console, for example, is like an app store for Kubernetes applications. You can use it to find and deploy databases, message queues, and other middleware—the kinds of components nearly all applications rely on. Like apps on your mobile device, Operators keep their applications running and updated with the latest features and fixes.

CI/CD: Pipelines

OpenShift brings the continuous integration and continuous development (CI/CD) system into the cluster. OpenShift's pipelines let you compose a process to build, test, package, and release your application. In this book, you'll go from logging in to the OpenShift Web Console to having the platform automatically build and deploy your code when you commit changes to your source repository. Once you establish deployment settings and build triggers, OpenShift should fade into the background of daily application development.

Networking and Service Mesh

OpenShift can simplify or even automate much of the tedious work of connecting application components together and to the outside world of your users and customers.

OpenShift Routes configure an included Layer 7 reverse proxy for external HTTP connections to internal, load-balancing cluster Services. A Service is a stable endpoint representing the running pods of an application, since those may come and go with scaling, failover, or upgrades. A route specifies the external DNS hostnames for which it relays traffic and the Service to which that traffic should be directed.

OpenShift also has a bolt-on service mesh, Istio (*https://istio.io*). A *service mesh* measures and controls how services connect with one another and the outside world. Istio detail is beyond the scope of this book, but once you've mastered deploying applications on OpenShift, you can learn more about service meshes and Istio in *Introducing Istio Service Mesh for Microservices* by Christian Posta and Burr Sutter (O'Reilly).

Integrated Prometheus Metrics, Monitoring, and Alerts

OpenShift constructs its features for monitoring cluster resources atop the open-source Prometheus (*https://prometheus.io*) project. The Web Console presents graphs showing CPU, memory, and network usage for the whole cluster, a project, a deployment, or all the way down to a running container. Figure 1-3 shows the CPU usage of a deployment.

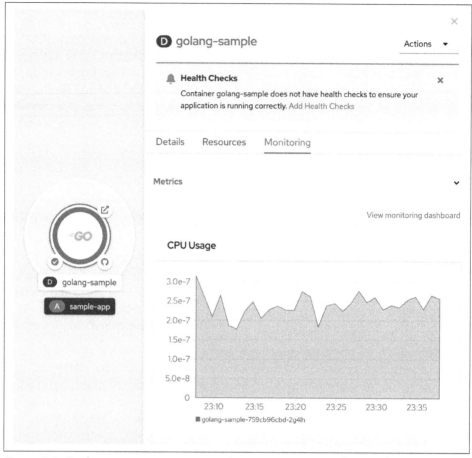

Figure 1-3. Deployment resource consumption monitoring in Web Console

OpenShift can gather application-specific metrics from programs that produce the standard Prometheus data format. Prometheus exporter libraries available for many languages equip an application to deliver statistics about its internal state in an interoperable way.

Summary

You've seen how OpenShift layers developer tools and application management atop Kubernetes to make it easier to deliver your software and keep it running. The next chapter introduces key concepts for building and deploying applications on OpenShift.

CHAPTER 2

OpenShift Concepts

OpenShift is a superset of Kubernetes. Kubernetes concepts, commands, and practices work on OpenShift. You can do any of the usual kubectl operations in the Open-Shift API. The reverse is not true. OpenShift has features and entire workflows that are not part of Kubernetes. For example, BuildConfig and Build resources in the OpenShift API represent the configuration and iterative executions of a process to build an application. They are not in the Kubernetes API, because Kubernetes doesn't define a mechanism for compiling software and assembling container images. Open-Shift adds these two types of resources and the facilities that use them. Likewise, while Kubernetes has a *namespace* to organize resources, OpenShift augments the namespace to form the *Project*. A Project demarcates access boundaries for clusters occupied by multiple tenants and serves as a discrete unit for administrative policy.

Kubernetes establishes the components of a container orchestrator and a way of addressing them. OpenShift builds on that foundation, adding tools and abstractions for the developers who build the apps that run on the cluster. Keeping those apps running is the reason the cluster exists.

This chapter introduces key concepts for building, deploying, and maintaining applications with OpenShift. It notes where these concepts extend or replace Kubernetes abstractions. We'll begin by explaining how OpenShift Projects extend the basic Kubernetes namespace.

Projects Organize Applications and Teams

The Kubernetes namespace defines a scope for resource names. A cluster may be divided into any number of namespaces. Within a namespace, the names of resources must be unique. Namespaces partition a cluster among multiple applications, multiple application layers, or multiple users. To enforce access control or any security among those namespaces requires additional pieces and policies. OpenShift's Project extends the basic namespace with default access controls (Figure 2-1).

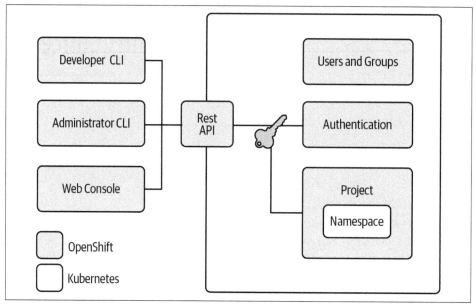

Figure 2-1. OpenShift Project: production-ready namespace

OpenShift enforces access control to the cluster and its resources. Details are beyond the scope of this book, but essentially, in OpenShift pluggable authentication modules govern authentification for an authorization regime built atop Kubernetes role-based access control (RBAC).

RBAC rules define a *user* and make the user a member of at least one *group*. Groups are used to represent teams or units within a company that might need different levels of access to different Projects. Your user and group determine what resources you can see and what you can do with them. Projects, then, can be used to divide the cluster among multiple teams or multiple applications, enforcing the rules that keep them from interfering in other Projects. You can assign roles and the rights they entail to individual users, and users inherit roles from their group memberships.

Projects and Applications

Is a Project the same thing as an "application"? Projects divide the cluster into functional units, but they leave the ontology up to a cluster's admins. On some clusters, a Project is dedicated to an application. Sometimes a Project is instead granted to a team, who might then run several applications in it, using labels to brand each application's resources. OpenShift provides convenience features to apply and employ these labels to sort multiple applications in a Project. For example, resource icons can be grouped together by application in an OpenShift Web Console Topology view, like the components of `sample-app` shown in Figure 2-2.

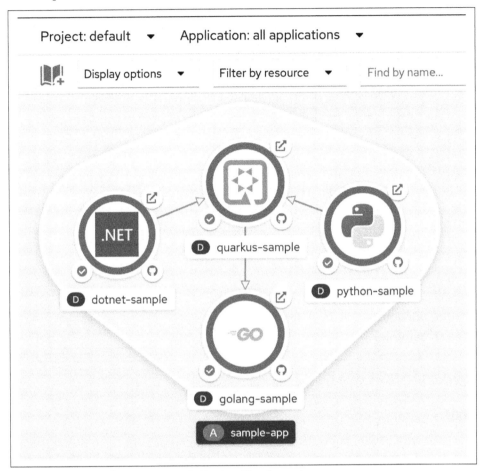

Figure 2-2. An application group in Project Topology view

Application Components in OpenShift

OpenShift represents an application as several abstractions, including the BuildConfig or pipeline for building that source and packaging the result in a container image, the configuration of how the running program should be deployed and scaled, and how it connects to the cluster's network and potentially onto the wider internet in Figure 2-3.

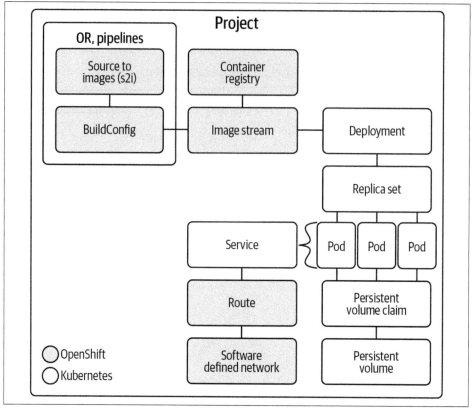

Figure 2-3. Application parts in an OpenShift Project

Pods

The basic unit of running code in any Kubernetes cluster is the *pod*. A pod groups one or more containers together and guarantees they all run on the same cluster node. A pod has a unique IP address within the cluster, shared by all the containers in it. Containers in a pod can also share persistent storage volumes and memory, and can communicate with one another over the localhost interface.

Pods are the unit of horizontal scaling. When a deployment is scaled up, new pods are created, usually on other cluster nodes. In a deployment's specification, these are called *replicas*. Each replicated pod has the same set of containers and configuration but its own local runtime state.

Services

Each pod in a set of replicas has a unique IP address that can be reached from within the cluster. But the pods could be scaled up or down or be replaced by new pods in a failure or a rolling application update. The cluster provides an indirection through which you can reach a dynamic set of replicas. This is the *Service* abstraction. A service has an IP address and DNS name in the cluster. Connections there are routed to one of the pods in the set, even as the pods in the set are scaled or replaced.

OpenShift Routes

A Kubernetes Service is a load-balanced endpoint representing a set of pods. Usually there is an application running in those pods providing a service of some kind. A Service has a DNS name resolving to an IP address within the cluster, so it is uncomplicated for other application components to connect to it. But that name and IP address are meaningless outside of the cluster. The rest of the office, the outside world, and the whole internet don't know anything about them. Something has to connect outside traffic to the cluster Service living in the cluster's logical network.

Kubernetes provides the *Ingress* resource (*https://oreil.ly/rVfKT*) to define the wiring of outside connections to the cluster's logical network. Ingress is a flexible, configurable representation of a network aperture and the rules under which it may be traversed. An Ingress resource requires an Ingress controller to satisfy its rules. An Ingress controller is a program that knows how to control an external network. There are Ingress controllers (*https://oreil.ly/6eKxj*) for reverse proxies, hardware load balancers, routers, and API-driven cloud provider networks, for example.

The OpenShift *Route* is a simplified way to expose the most common HTTP and HTTPS services to networks outside the cluster. Creating a route associated with a Service causes OpenShift to configure its included reverse proxy with a DNS name and an IP address reachable from an external network. Connections to the route's external IP address are then forwarded to the cluster Service, and from there on to an application pod.

Building Container Images

Before a pod fields requests coming in through a route to a Service, you must build the application. An OpenShift *BuildConfig* describes how to combine source code with a "base image" to create a new application container image. The base image usually contains the tools for building source code in some programming language or framework. For example, there are Builder Images for common languages such as Java, Python, Go, and PHP. A BuildConfig can respond to webhooks, triggering builds in automatic response to changes to their base image or source code.

Deploying Applications

An application is built to be deployed. OpenShift's *Deployment* defines the template from which new pods are stamped and the rules for recycling those pods when their configuration or their container image changes. For example, a deployment can begin a rolling update of its pods to deploy a new container image when a new build is triggered by a source code commit, or when a security update to a distribution requires a new base image. A deployment usually represents a single service or application component.

Interacting with OpenShift

There is more than one tool for using OpenShift, and the tools are different in their capabilities and intended users. All of the tools, however, are the same in how they talk to a cluster: through the OpenShift API. The Kubernetes core presents, and OpenShift extends, a REST API (*https://oreil.ly/MUj6p*). In fact, any network client can communicate with the API, given authorized access and the OpenShift API reference documentation (*https://oreil.ly/HZQCC*). This book does not go into detail on the subject, but API access is useful for integrating with external systems; for example, an existing container-building process.

oc

The oc command-line tool is an OpenShift API client. It's one of the main ways of interacting with an OpenShift cluster. Based on the same *client-go* library as the standard Kubernetes API client, kubectl, oc speaks all the kubectl commands as well as the superset of commands specific to OpenShift. While kubectl can scale a replica set to more pods, it doesn't know anything about the OpenShift Routes you'll soon use to connect outside traffic to your applications, for example. oc understands both, including the other important developer-oriented features like on-cluster builds, image streams, and the Projects that organize them.

OpenShift Web Console

The other tool you'll get cozy with in this book is the OpenShift Web Console, a graphical environment for deploying, managing, and monitoring your applications on OpenShift. The Web Console lets you see how application parts relate and how they consume cluster resources with topographical representations, graphs, and visual connections.

Summary

Now that you understand the relationship between OpenShift's developer features and its Kubernetes core, you're ready to put them to work. You need an OpenShift cluster to conquer the exercises throughout the rest of the book. That's why the next chapter shows you how to get one.

CHAPTER 3

OpenShift Lab

You need an OpenShift cluster to complete the exercises throughout the rest of the book. This chapter explains how to run OpenShift in a virtual machine (VM) on your computer and introduces the basics of interacting with it. It also suggests other ways to access a cluster if you can't run OpenShift locally.

OpenShift runs on your laptop, on a brigade of aging computers in the home lab of one of this book's authors, on premises in data centers, and in public clouds. You can step through the examples in this book on any OpenShift cluster of recent vintage, meaning version 4.7 or later. If you don't already have access to a cluster, this chapter will show you how to set up an OpenShift VM on your computer.

CodeReady Containers

For the scenarios in this book, we recommend using CodeReady Containers (CRC), an OpenShift 4 cluster that runs on your local computer in a single VM. This cluster provides a minimal environment for developing and testing purposes, including everything you need to get started.

The CRC VM is considered a minimal environment because the monitoring and machine-config operators within the cluster are disabled to conserve resources. Unfortunately, this means that all of the various performance monitoring charts within the Web Console are presented as blank space. And of course, CRC is a single-node "cluster," so it can only emulate multinode scaling or rolling upgrades.

The CRC cluster uses an internal virtual network on your local machine. The IP address of the VM may vary from deployment to deployment, but your configuration will be displayed after OpenShift is deployed. You can always print the current cluster's configuration with the command `crc console --credentials`.

CRC Requirements

CRC requires a few things from a hardware and operating system perspective in order to run. If you cannot satisfy these requirements, it may be possible to run on the book scenarios an existing OpenShift cluster, but we have not tested those environments.

CRC requires at least the following system resources:

- 4 virtual CPUs (vCPUs)
- 9 GB of free memory
- 35 GB of storage space

Be sure to provide at least the minimum requirements and, if possible, use hardware that exceeds these specifications. The CRC VM is a single-node OpenShift cluster and requires a powerful machine to run.

The OpenShift Lab has been tested on relatively generous laptops with Intel i7 CPUs or similar, with 16 GiB of memory, but be prepared for some latency. In these situations we suggest allocating $n - 1$ CPU resources, where n is equal to the number of cores on your system. In addition to the CPU resource allocation, we recommend allocating at least 12 of the machine's 16 GiB of memory to the CRC VM, connecting to AC power and closing all unrelated programs.

CRC runs on Windows, macOS, and Linux and has specific requirements for each. You will likely need administrative privileges on your local computer to set up CRC.

CRC Operating System Requirements

Windows
> Windows 10 Fall Creators Update (version 1709) or newer; Windows 10 Home Edition is not supported.

macOS
> OS X 10.4 Mojave or newer

Linux
> Officially supported on Red Hat Enterprise Linux/CentOS 7.5 or newer, or the latest two stable Fedora releases

---

While the following steps will walk you through configuring CRC on Windows, CRC also supports Mac and Linux operating systems. It is always a good idea to check out the CodeReady documentation for updated and specific instructions for your system. You can do that on the CRC website (*https://oreil.ly/m64rY*).

Installing CRC on Windows

To install CRC on Windows:

1. Head to Red Hat OpenShift Cluster Manager (*https://oreil.ly/2iEgH*) and log in to your Red Hat account (Figure 3-1). Create an account for free if you do not already have one.

Figure 3-1. OpenShift Cluster Manager login

2. In the Cluster Manager (Figure 3-2), download the latest version of CRC for your operating system and download your pull secret. The pull secret encodes your CRC license entitlement for CRC and OpenShift components retrieved from Red Hat repositories.

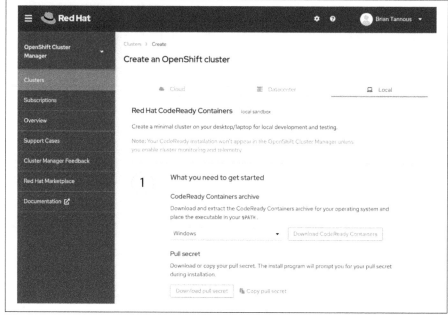

Figure 3-2. OpenShift Cluster Manager

3. Extract the CRC archive and navigate to the extracted folder in a PowerShell terminal:

```
PS C:\Users\Brian\CRC\crc-windows> ls


    Directory: C:\Users\Brian\CRC\crc-windows


Mode                 LastWriteTime         Length Name
----                 -------------         ------ ----
------         4/12/2021  10:00 AM     2490319884 crc.exe
------         4/12/2021  10:00 AM         406768 doc.pdf
------         4/12/2021  10:00 AM          10759 LICENSE
```

4. Install the `crc` command on your machine by placing it within your terminal session's `path`.

 Refer to the CRC installation documentation for more information on how to do this for your specific operating system.

5. Run `crc setup`. You will likely need to provide administrative access. Be sure to read the command's output, as the logs might mention that you need to reboot to continue.

   a. (Optional) If you needed to reboot your machine, run `crc setup` again in a PowerShell terminal to continue the setup process:

   ```
   PS> crc setup
   INFO Checking if admin-helper executable is cached
   INFO Checking minimum RAM requirements
   [...]
   INFO Extracting embedded bundle crc_hyperv_4.7.5.crcbundle to C:\Use...
   INFO Uncompressing crc_hyperv_4.7.5.crcbundle
   ```

6. Now that your local machine is configured to run CRC, run `crc start --help` to see all of the available configuration switches:

   ```
   PS > crc start --help
   Usage:
     crc start [flags]

   Flags:
     -b, --bundle string            The system bundle used for deployment
                                    of the OpenShift cluster (default "C:\\
                                    Users\\Brian\\.crc\\cache\\
                                    crc_hyperv_4.7.5.crcbundle")
     -c, --cpus int                 Number of CPU cores to allocate
                                    to the OpenShift cluster (default 4)
         --disable-update-check     Don't check for update
     -d, --disk-size uint           Total size in GiB of the disk used by
                                    the OpenShift cluster (default 31)
     -h, --help                     help for start
     -m, --memory int               MiB of memory to allocate to the
                                    OpenShift cluster (default 9216)
     -n, --nameserver string        IPv4 address of nameserver to use for
                                    the OpenShift cluster
     -o, --output string            Output format. One of: json
     -p, --pull-secret-file string  File path of image pull secret
                                    (download from  ...)

   Global Flags:
         --log-level string    log level (e.g. "debug | info | warn | error")
                               (default "info")
   ```

7. Now you can start CRC by specifying at least the default 4-vCPU and 9 GiB memory configuration.

   Execute `crc start -p pull-secret.txt -m 9216 -c 4`:

   ```
   PS > crc start -p C:\Users\Brian\CRC\pull-secret.txt -m 9216 -c 4
   INFO Checking if podman remote executable is cached
   INFO Checking if admin-helper executable is cached
   ```

```
INFO Checking minimum RAM requirements
INFO Checking if running in a shell with administrator rights
INFO Checking Windows 10 release
[…]
INFO All operators are available. Ensuring stability ...
INFO Operators are stable (2/3) ...
INFO Operators are stable (3/3) ...
INFO Adding crc-admin and crc-developer contexts to kubeconfig...
Started the OpenShift cluster.
[… Continued below]
```

CRC Always Wants More

The OpenShift cluster requires at least these minimums to run in the CRC VM. Some workloads may need more resources. We suggest assigning as much as possible while not constraining your host workstation. For example, avoid most shortages by running CRC on a powerful machine and configuring the VM with 20 GiB of memory and six CPU cores.

You can increase the memory allocated to the CRC VM by providing crc start with the argument -m <memory>, where memory is a value in MiB, usually a power of two. Start the VM with 20 GiB of RAM by issuing a command like crc start -m 20480, for instance. Set the number of CPU cores for the CRC VM by adding the argument -c <number of vCPUs>.

One workaround for constrained systems might be to configure CRC as a headless server and then connecting to it from a second machine, dedicating to CRC nearly all of the resources of the first machine. You can learn more about remoting to CRC on the OpenShift blog (*https://oreil.ly/nBlJL*).

CLI How-To: Common CRC Life Cycle Tasks

The crc console --credentials command will return the credentials for the CRC machine as well as the URL for accessing the Web Console.

To check the status of the CRC machine, use the command crc status. If you need to stop the OpenShift VM while saving your progress, you can run the command crc stop.

To start a stopped CRC machine and continue where you left off, run the command crc start. *Note: This command will create a new CRC VM if one does not exist.*

To clean up and completely remove your CRC cluster and VM, use crc cleanup.

Run crc help for a complete and always current guide to its subcommands.

Logging In to OpenShift

Now that the OpenShift cluster has started, you can log in. You probably noticed that the tail of the output from the `crc start` command showed the Web Console URL along with authentication credentials for both an administrator and a typical user:

```
The server is accessible via web console at:
  https://console-openshift-console.apps-crc.testing

Log in as administrator:
  Username: kubeadmin
  Password: un1Q-g3n3r8d # Note: Your password will be different.

Log in as user:
  Username: developer
  Password: developer

Use the 'oc' command line interface:
  PS> & crc oc-env | Invoke-Expression
  PS> oc login -u developer https://api.crc.testing:6443
```

Log In to the Web Console

Use the printed username and password pairs to access your new OpenShift cluster (*https://console-openshift-console.apps-crc.testing*).

Go to the Web Console of your OpenShift instance at the URL in your terminal output and log in using the administrator credentials printed by the `crc start` command or at any time by invoking `crc console --credentials` (Figure 3-3).

Figure 3-3. OpenShift Web Console login

OpenShift Web Console

The Administrator perspective of the OpenShift Web Console will allow you to handle all administrative tasks within the OpenShift cluster, such as working with users, nodes, workloads, and networking (Figure 3-4).

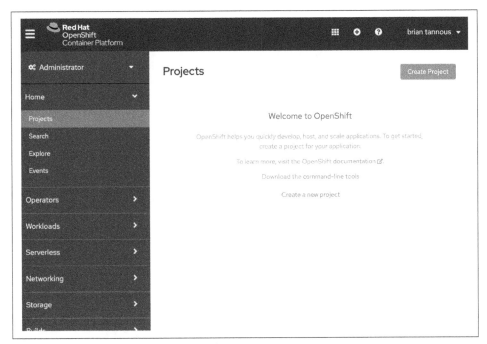

Figure 3-4. OpenShift Web Console Administrator perspective

Developer Web Console

While technically you could accomplish deployments and builds of your application from within the Administrator perspective of the OpenShift Web Console, we will be working primarily in the Developer perspective. Switch perspectives by clicking on the upper-left dropdown and choosing Developer (Figure 3-5).

Figure 3-5. Web Console perspectives

Here you will see the Developer console that you will primarily be interacting with throughout the book. This console allows you to handle developer-related tasks such as deploying, building, and monitoring your application (Figure 3-6).

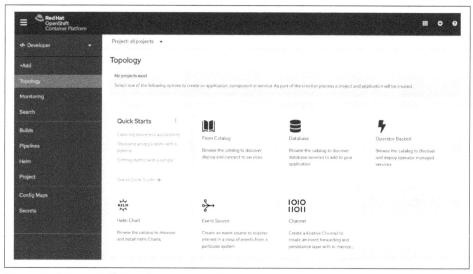

Figure 3-6. OpenShift Developer perspective

Log In on the Command Line

As we discussed in Chapter 2, the command-line interface for OpenShift is oc.

The output of the crc start command has the information on how to get started and log in with oc:

```
Use the 'oc' command line interface:
  PS> & crc oc-env | Invoke-Expression
  PS> oc login -u developer https://api.crc.testing:6443

  PS> oc whoami
  developer
  PS> oc get nodes
  [...]
```

It is generally best to match oc versions to OpenShift server versions. Since you are using CRC to launch this specific version of OpenShift, we used the built-in version of oc set with the & crc oc-env | Invoke-Expression command. You can check that the versions of the client and server match with oc version:

```
PS> oc version
Client Version: 4.7.5
Server Version: 4.7.5
Kubernetes Version: v1.20.0+5fbfd19
```

You can also download the oc command-line tool by clicking on the question mark (?) icon on the top-right corner of the OpenShift Web Console and choosing Command Line Tools from the menu (Figure 3-7).

Visual Studio Code: OpenShift Connector

Now that CRC is ready to go, you might want to check out the OpenShift Connector for Visual Studio Code, especially if you happen to already be a VS coder. This extension adds features in VS Code to easily create, deploy, and debug your application on OpenShift. You can also use it to set up and start CRC.

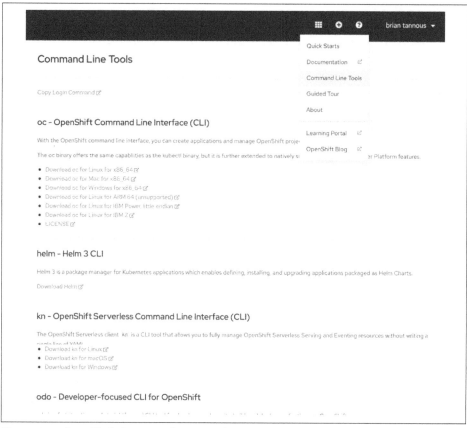

Figure 3-7. OpenShift Command Line Tools

Summary

In this chapter, you set up CRC so that you have access to a local OpenShift cluster. You also logged in to the cluster with both the Web Console and the command-line oc utility. You explored two of the common user roles in OpenShift, and surveyed the Developer and Administrator perspectives in the Web Console. Now that you have a running cluster, let's get something deployed!

CHAPTER 4

Deploying an Application on OpenShift

You've got a handle on OpenShift concepts and you have access to an OpenShift cluster. Now you'll use OpenShift to create a project, build the project's application from source, and run it.

A Simple Sample Application

We will honor tech tradition by beginning with a "Hello World" program. This chapter's simple program runs an HTTP service that prints a response to each request. We've selected the Go programming language because it compiles quickly and to demonstrate more than one language environments. You'll use the Java Quarkus framework to build a more complex application in later chapters. OpenShift techniques you'll use throughout the book, like on-cluster builds and automatic deployment, are largely agnostic about the language and frameworks you choose for a project.

First, get a copy of the source code for the Hello World application. You'll use Git (*http://git-scm.com*) to manage the source and GitHub (*https://github.com*) to make your copy available for your cluster to build. Point your browser to this chapter's GitHub repository (*https://oreil.ly/QVVNi*). Fork a copy to your own GitHub account with the Fork button at the top right. In Git terms, a "fork" is an exact copy of a repository at a point in time. You can modify your fork to create your own version or to make, test, and submit changes back to the original repo. You'll use Git in this chapter, but you don't need deep Git expertise; the following extremely brief overview of Git words and ways should get you started.

Git and GitHub

Git is a system for distributed version control. Usually, a Git repository on your computer will store the working copies of your source code. You'll use the `git` tool to `commit` changes there, then `push` the repository somewhere, or collaborate with an upstream repo with change proposals referred to as *pull requests*. This decentralized operation is the "distributed" part.

In this book, you'll push source code to GitHub, a social network for source code. The "social" part means other people and, more importantly for your project, other systems can connect to, copy, work with, and propose changes to your source code stored on GitHub. GitHub also has browser-based tools for editing source and committing changes, and in this chapter you'll use those so that you can play the first few levels of OpenShift without a side quest into the command line.

Building and Deploying the Application on OpenShift

The first thing you need is an OpenShift Project to contain the application resources. Log in to your CRC cluster web console (*https://console-openshift-console.apps-crc.testing*). There, the default account is "developer" and the password is also "developer".

Make sure you're using the Developer perspective by checking or changing the selection to Developer using the OpenShift perspective switcher dropdown in the upper-left corner. Click on Topology. Create a new project by clicking the Project: All Projects dropdown and then click Create Project (Figure 4-1).

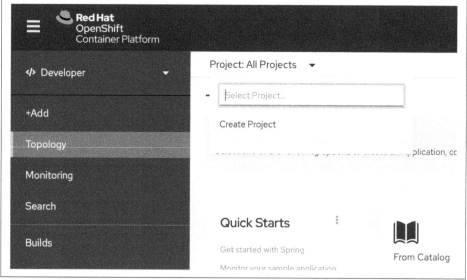

Figure 4-1. OpenShift Web Console: Project dropdown

In the Create Project dialog, configure the new Project, as shown in Figure 4-2.

Create Project

Name *

o4d-hello

Display Name

Hello OpenShift for Developers

Description

The hello world application for the book OpenShift for Developers|

[Cancel] [Create]

Figure 4-2. Creating a new Project

CLI How-To: Create a New Project

Create a new Project in the OpenShift CLI by executing the following code:

```
oc new-project \
--display-name='Hello OpenShift for Developers' \
--description='hello world' \
o4d-hello
```

Since you haven't deployed anything, the Topology view will try to help out with a grid of things you might want to deploy. Choose From Git.

The console will present a Git build configuration dialog, similar to that seen in Figure 4-3. Enter the URL of your forked Hello World source in your GitHub account: for example, *https://github.com/<your-name>/hello.git*. When you do, OpenShift will check the contents of the repository and, for known languages, will automatically select the appropriate Builder Image containing the compiler and other tools to build it.

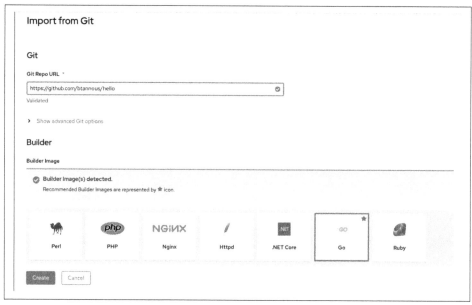

Figure 4-3. Configuring a build from Go source code in the OpenShift Web Console

Check that Go is selected in the grid of Builder Images offered in the dialog. Otherwise, accept the defaults and click Create.

CLI How-To: Create a New Go Application

It is possible to create the hello deployment using the command line by executing the following:

```
oc new-app golang~https://github.com/<your-name>/hello.git
```

When you click Create, OpenShift will start building your source code with the Go compiler tools of the selected Builder Image. You'll be returned to the console's Topology view, which shows the application and updates its display as it builds and deploys (Figure 4-4).

The application's Topology icon conveys key information. Mouse over the badges on the icon's edge and you'll see that you can click through to build status, directly to the Git repository URL with the app's source code, or to the external URL of a route to the application (Figure 4-5).

Figure 4-4. Topology view with Hello World application

Figure 4-5. Topology icon Route badge

The status of the deployment is conveyed by different colors and tool tips. Dark blue indicates a running application, light blue one that is not yet ready, and red an application that needs attention because errors have occurred.

Click the Route badge to open the application's external URL in your web browser (Figure 4-6).

Hello OpenShift for Developers!

Figure 4-6. HTTP response printed by the Hello World application

CLI How-To: List Routes in a Project

List the routes in a Project on the command line by running `oc get routes`.

Adding and Deploying a New Feature

Starting with a few lines of source code, you've used OpenShift to fetch, build, and deploy a stateless web application of contrived simplicity. Now imagine you are assigned a ticket for a feature request: change the displayed text to "Hello World!". You can make this change and then have OpenShift rebuild the application and deploy the result, replacing the previous version.

This basic loop prepares you for two key ideas in the more elaborate application you'll build through the rest of the book. The source-to-image build system on Open‐ Shift will form the core of the more complete deployment pipeline you'll create in Chapter 6. In later chapters, you'll see how to set and change deployment strategies to keep services available during redeployments, or to deploy a new application version to only a subset of replicas, for single-cluster A/B testing.

Changing hello source

To address the text-change ticket, you need to change a string in the application source. If you're a Git veteran, you may have cloned the repo to your local machine, and you already know how to edit with your preferred tool, commit, and push back to your GitHub repo. If that process isn't familiar to you, don't worry; for now, the needed change is simple enough to do it quickly in the GitHub web editor, and we will show you how to clone, change, commit, and send your changes back to your publicly visible GitHub repository before you need to do more involved coding.

Open the Go source file for your Hello World application, *hello-openshift-for-developers.go*, in your browser. Your copy will be at *https://github.com/<your-name>/hello/blob/master/hello-openshift-for-developers.go*. You will see the code shown in Figure 4-7.

```
36 lines (30 sloc)    647 Bytes

  1   package main
  2
  3   import (
  4           "fmt"
  5           "net/http"
  6           "os"
  7   )
  8
  9   func helloHandler(w http.ResponseWriter, r *http.Request) {
 10           response := os.Getenv("RESPONSE")
 11           if len(response) == 0 {
 12                   response = "Hello OpenShift for Developers!"
 13           }
 14
 15           fmt.Fprintln(w, response)
 16           fmt.Println("Servicing an impatient beginner's request.")
 17   }
```

Figure 4-7. Existing GitHub source view of Hello World Go source

Click the pencil icon at the top right of the source view (Figure 4-8) to enter editor mode.

Figure 4-8. GitHub pencil icon

Then find the string `Hello OpenShift for Developers!` and change it to `Hello World!`, as shown in Figure 4-9.

```
<> Edit file      ⊙ Preview changes

 1    package main
 2
 3    import (
 4            "fmt"
 5            "net/http"
 6            "os"
 7    )
 8
 9    func helloHandler(w http.ResponseWriter, r *http.Request) {
10            response := os.Getenv("RESPONSE")
11            if len(response) == 0 {
12                    response = "Hello World!"
13            }
14
```

Figure 4-9. Edited GitHub source view of Hello World Go source

Finally, save the changes to the main branch of your application repo. It's good practice to provide a pithy commit message explaining the change, with a subject and
body similar to an email, as shown in Figure 4-10. Click "Commit changes" to commit your changes.

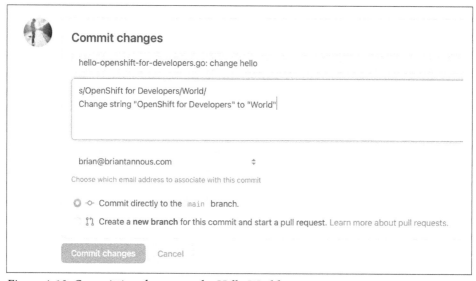

Figure 4-10. Committing changes to the Hello World repo

A new OpenShift Deployment

An OpenShift BuildConfig represents a source code location and a process for building it into a deployable container. You already have a BuildConfig, created for building the Hello World app and reused each time a new release is deployed. Open the

Builds view from the left menu of the Web Console's Developer perspective. Then click on the `hello-git` BuildConfig to open it (Figure 4-11).

Figure 4-11. OpenShift hello-git BuildConfig

Start a build with the "Start build" item from the Actions menu at top right (Figure 4-12).

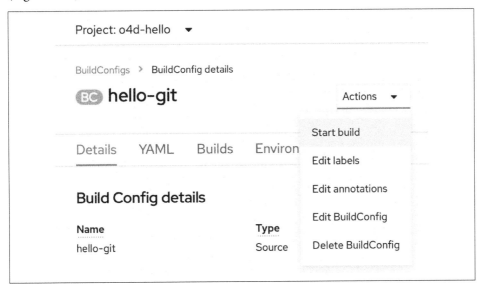

Figure 4-12. Actions menu: "Start build" item

CLI How-To: Start a Build from an Existing BuildConfig

It is possible to start the `hello-git` build using the command line by executing `oc start-build hello-git`.

As shown in Figure 4-13, when the build completes, clicking on the URL icon in the Topology view will open the latest version of your application in a browser tab. Hello World!

Hello World!

Figure 4-13. Application feature request ticket closed

Summary

Believe it or not, you've just mastered the key pieces of deploying your code on Open-Shift. From source to build to rollout and a changeset in between, once configured, OpenShift assumed the "ops" chores and let you concentrate on the "dev" part. In Chapter 5, you'll expand on the build concept with the more capable and modular OpenShift Pipelines, creating a CD process for a more complete and realistic application with multiple components and persistent state.

CHAPTER 5

OpenShift Pipelines

OpenShift Pipelines is a CI/CD system based on the open source Tekton project. With Pipelines, you can trigger repeatable builds when source code changes, integrate tests into the process, and configure automatic redeployment strategies, from rolling updates to traffic-splitting A/B testing on a single cluster.

In this chapter, you'll see how Pipelines integrates Tekton fundamentals with Open-Shift to make it easier to create and manage stepwise build and deployment processes. You'll add the Pipelines Operator to your OpenShift cluster. Then you'll be ready to create a pipeline to build, test, and deploy a realistic application with multiple compo-nents, which you'll iterate on to add features and fix bugs throughout the rest of the book.

Tekton

Tekton lets you create pipelines of repeatable steps. Tekton steps happen in a pod specifically created for the task. Tekton tasks are therefore isolated from one another and from the rest of the cluster, but you don't have to manage a dedicated build server. Tekton's moving parts are Kubernetes resources, so you can use familiar tools to create, manage, and monitor Tekton pipelines.

Tekton is the foundation of OpenShift Pipelines. Pipelines make it easier to set up, run, and monitor build processes by bundling the essential Tekton components and adding management tools in line with OpenShift conventions, including graphical representations of pipelines in the Web Console. You'll see the two terms used inter-changeably in this book, in Pipelines documentation, and in OpenShift CLI and GUI elements as well.

OpenShift Pipelines Operator

The OpenShift Pipelines Operator installs and manages Pipelines components and services. This includes automatically updating Pipelines as new versions are released.

Installing the Pipelines Operator

Log in to the Web Console with an account granted `cluster-admin` or enough equivalent rights to install and manage Operators. On CRC, you were issued a cluster-admin username and password when you ran `crc start`. The username is usually `kubeadmin`; your password for it is generated and unique. If you don't remember the password generated for your cluster's `kubeadmin` account, you can recover it with the command `crc console --credentials`.

OperatorHub

The OperatorHub is a catalog of available Operators in the OpenShift Web Console Administrator view. Administrators establish a subscription to an Operator in the OperatorHub, after which the application or service that the Operator manages is available for instantiation in one or more cluster namespaces. You'll use the OperatorHub to find and install the Red Hat OpenShift Pipelines Operator. Then you'll switch back to your developer role and create and run an actual pipeline.

> Check out the Kubernetes community's home to share Operators for use on OpenShift, OKD, or Kubernetes (*https://operatorhub.io*). If you have a commercial application that you want to make accessible to your customers, get it included in the OpenShift OperatorHub using the certification workflow provided on the Red Hat Partner Connect portal (*https://connect.redhat.com*).

First, make sure you're in the Administrator perspective by checking or changing the selection at the top left of the console. Click on Operators and then OperatorHub in the left menu. Search for "pipelines", as shown in Figure 5-1.

Figure 5-1. Pipelines in OperatorHub

Install the Red Hat OpenShift Pipelines Operator

Click the Red Hat OpenShift Pipelines card. You'll see the install configuration screen for Pipelines as shown in Figure 5-2. Note that the Pipelines version on your Open-Shift cluster will likely be newer than the version 1.4.1 shown in the figure.

CLI How-To: Install the OpenShift Pipelines Operator

You can install the OpenShift Pipelines Operator via the command line using a little bit of YAML:

```
cat <<EOF | kubectl apply -f -
apiVersion: operators.coreos.com/v1alpha1
kind: Subscription
metadata:
  name: openshift-pipelines-operator
  namespace: openshift-operators
spec:
  channel:  stable
  name: openshift-pipelines-operator-rh
  source: redhat-operators
  sourceNamespace: openshift-marketplace
EOF
```

Accept the defaults selected on the Install screen. The default settings make pipelines available in all namespaces, with automatic updates managed by the Pipelines

Operator. OpenShift Pipelines is ready to go when the status dialog shows "Installed Operator - Ready for use".

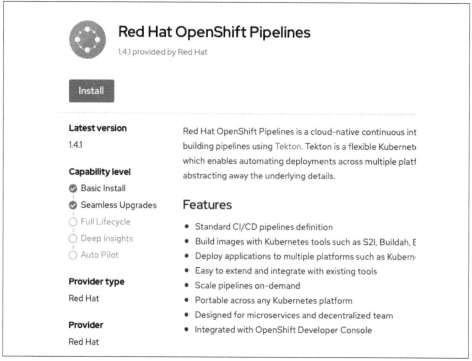

Figure 5-2. Red Hat OpenShift Pipelines install configuration

Pipelines in the Web Console

Once the Operator is installed, you can see the high-level Administrator perspective view of the APIs through which you can manipulate pipelines. Click on Installed Operators in the left navigation pane, and then click on the Red Hat OpenShift Pipelines Operator (Figure 5-3).

You can also see the same APIs that Tekton provides using the OpenShift command line:

```
$ oc api-resources --api-group=tekton.dev
NAME              SHORTNAMES   APIVERSION            NAMESPACED   KIND
clustertasks                   tekton.dev/v1beta1    false ClusterTask
conditions                     tekton.dev/v1alpha1   true  Condition
pipelineresources              tekton.dev/v1alpha1   true  PipelineResource
pipelineruns      pr,prs       tekton.dev/v1beta1    true  PipelineRun
pipelines                      tekton.dev/v1beta1    true  Pipeline
runs                           tekton.dev/v1alpha1   true  Run
taskruns          tr,trs       tekton.dev/v1beta1    true  TaskRun
tasks                          tekton.dev/v1beta1    true  Task
```

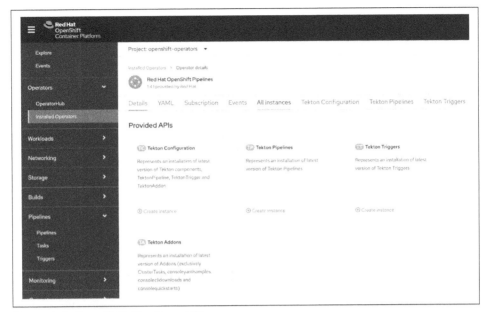

Figure 5-3. OpenShift Pipelines APIs

Using Pipelines

In the Web Console Developer perspective, you can create pipeline tasks and select reusable tasks to form pipelines, then run and observe them, check their log output, and control them graphically. On the command line, you drive pipelines with the OpenShift `oc` tool and a specific utility for pipelines called `tkn`. The `tkn` and `oc` command-line utilities are available in the OpenShift web user interface. Click the question mark icon near your username at the top-right corner and then select Command Line Tools, as shown in Figure 5-4, to access download links for both tools for the three most popular operating systems.

 If you are a VS coder, be sure to check out the extension for Tekton Pipelines in addition to the OpenShift Connector for Visual Studio Code that we mentioned in Chapter 3. This extension allows you to graphically build a pipeline, and it connects to Tekton Hub for reusable pipelines and tasks shared by the community.

Figure 5-4. OpenShift command-line tools available in the Web Console

OpenShift Pipelines Resources

Tekton constructs pipelines from a list of Tasks, and therefore the Task is the basic unit of OpenShift Pipelines as well. A Task contains one or more steps. A Task occupies a pod, and each of its steps runs as a container in that pod. Tasks execute steps in serial order, starting each step on the completion of the one before it. A pipeline executes a set of these Tasks. Unlike the steps within them, all of a pipeline's Tasks run at once in parallel unless a Task is configured to wait on another. A PipelineRun represents a single execution of a pipeline. Each run can be configured with parameters read from the environment or from programmatic input (Figure 5-5).

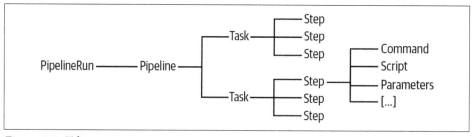

Figure 5-5. Tekton taxonomy

A Step is a series of commands that achieve a specific goal, such as building an image. Each Step runs sequentially in its own container inside a Task's pod. Since the containers in a pod can optionally share resources, Steps in a Task can use common shared volumes, ConfigMaps, and Secrets.

Command

A command is a sequence of a named executable, any subcommand, and its arguments. In the following code for a command called `generate`, the command to run is the `s2i` Source-to-Image utility. This example command gives `s2i`'s `build` subcommand the `--image-scripts-url` argument with a filepath. It also references a parameter, the `$PATH_CONTEXT`, to set its value to the `openjdk` image:

```
- name: generate
  command:
    - s2i
    - build
    - $(params.PATH_CONTEXT)
    - registry.access.redhat.com/redhat-openjdk-18/openjdk18-openshift
    - '--image-scripts-url'
    - 'image:///usr/local/s2i'
```

Script

A script puts an executable script inline so that a single Step that must run several operations can be more readably defined. An executable script can specify a command shell like `bash` or any language interpreter, such as `python3` in the following example:

```
- name: lint-markdown
  script:|-
    #!/usr/bin/env python3
    ...
```

Pipelines use other custom and native resources, like PersistentVolumes and claims, along with a set of parameters allowing for data persistence configuration of programs and scripts running in Steps or even between pod-isolated Tasks. Still, this look at the main elements should give you enough traction to apply pipelines in the next chapter to build an application with multiple components.

Summary

You've installed the OpenShift Pipelines Operator on your cluster. You're ready to create pipelines to build, test, and package the application you'll work on throughout the rest of the book. You met the open source Tekton system underpinning Pipelines, and you learned about a handful of the key resources in an OpenShift pipeline. Along the way, you got a glimpse of how Operators make it easier to install and manage foundation software and cluster services. In Chapter 6, you'll start developing a multitiered application and create a pipeline to build it from source.

Developing and Deploying from Source Code

Now that your local OpenShift has OpenShift Pipelines installed, you're ready to deploy a multitier application. This app is more complex than your initial "Hello World" service from Chapter 4, as it has two components that need to communicate. The app also has been designed to eventually incorporate a database, as you will see in Chapter 7. You will hand some of these complexities off to a pipeline to automate some of the repetitive tasks of building and rebuilding the application through several iterations.

Noted: A Cloud-Ready Notes Application

Noted is a simple note board where each note contains a title and some content. When an optional database is connected, it will allow you to maintain the list of prior posts and delete them. It consists of two main components, a frontend and a backend, similar to how a typical web application might be architected.

The frontend is written in Node.js and uses the React library to display the list of posts. The posts call the quarkus-backend REST endpoint at /posts. While you will not be editing the frontend component of the app, you can find the source code for the frontend app on GitHub (*https://oreil.ly/RmsiM*).

The backend is written using Quarkus, a Kubernetes-native Java stack for microservices and serverless development with fast startup times, hot reloads, a small memory footprint, and compact applications. The backend provides the /posts REST endpoint to the frontend app. Right now the lists of posts is volatile, stored only in memory. In Chapter 7, you'll modify the quarkus-backend to use a database to maintain the post list.

Application Topology

The easiest way to see the connectivity among components is through a topology view of the application (Figure 6-1).

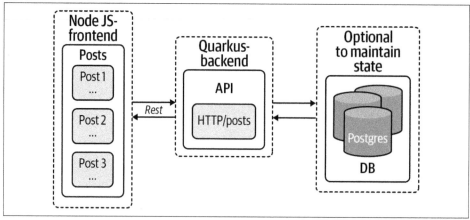

Figure 6-1. Noted topology

Figure 6-2 shows the primary pipeline used to clone both the frontend and backend source code repositories, build the applications into images, and deploy them on your local OpenShift cluster.

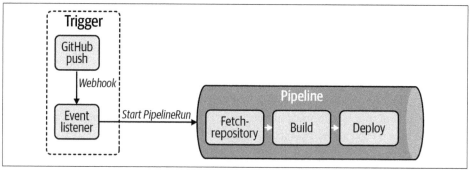

Figure 6-2. Noted pipeline

In Chapter 4, you deployed an application using the s2i build tooling in OpenShift. With OpenShift Pipelines, the build task will use buildah, and the deploy task will use the OpenShift CLI tool oc to handle deploying the image from OpenShift's internal registry. However, your pipeline will be extensible, allowing integration of commonly used services like GitHub and Slack. It will also handle other tasks that Tekton can run. Check out Tekton Hub (*https://hub.tekton.dev*) for some community-shared reusable tasks and pipelines.

Fork the Backend Repository

Before you deploy the application, you need to set up the GitHub repository for the quarkus-backend component. Open the book's quarkus-backend repo and fork the repository by clicking the Fork button at the top-right corner, as in Chapter 4.

Create a New Project for the Noted App

Now that you have your Git repository, you can deploy the frontend and backend components to OpenShift:

1. First, be sure you are logged in as a developer in the upper-right corner. If you are not logged in as a developer, log out and log in using the username and the password: *developer* as both.

2. Next, open the Developer console's Topology view in your browser.

3. Create a new Project by clicking the dropdown next to the currently selected project and then by clicking Create Project, as shown in Figure 6-3.

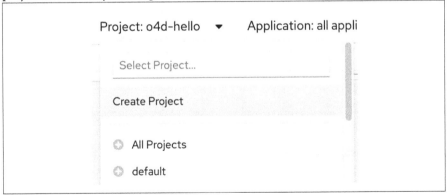

Figure 6-3. Creating a new Project for the Noted application

4. Configure the new Project as follows:

- Name: o4d-noted
- Display Name: OpenShift for Developers note
- Description: The Noted Application for the OpenShift for Developers Book

Deploy the Backend Component

Now deploy the quarkus-backend component to the new Project by clicking the Add from Git tile. The main branch is what you will initially deploy, which is configured to operate without a database.

Next, configure the new application component. For the Git Repo URL, enter **https://github.com/<your-name>/quarkus-backend.git**. Click on "Show advanced Git options"; for "Git reference," enter **main**; and for "Context dir," enter **/**. Leave the Source Secret box empty. See Figure 6-4.

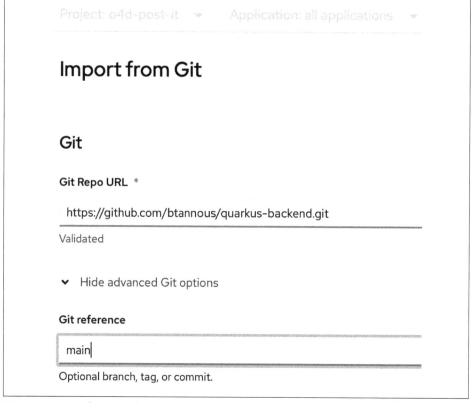

Figure 6-4. Configuring the quarkus-backend deployment

A *source secret* is used if you are working with a private registry and you need to specify some secret such as an ssh key. See the CI/CD section of the OpenShift documentation (*https://oreil.ly/1TunK*) for more details.

Continue configuring the quarkus-backend deployment. For Builder, make sure Java is selected. Under General, enter **noted** for the "Application name" and **quarkus-backend** for the Name (this is important for frontend/backend connectivity). Under Resources, make sure Deployment is selected. See Figure 6-5.

Project: o4d-post-it   ▾   Application: all applications   ▾

General

Application name

post-it

A unique name given to the Application grouping to label your resources.

Name *

quarkus-backend

A unique name given to the component that will be used to name associated resources.

Resources

Select the resource type to generate

◉ Deployment

apps/Deployment

A Deployment enables declarative updates for Pods and ReplicaSets.

Figure 6-5. Configuring the General and Resources sections of the quarkus-backend deployment

Continue to configure the quarkus-backend app by quickly adding a pipeline to build it from the source repository. Under Pipelines, check the "Add pipeline" checkbox. And under "Advanced options," uncheck the Create a Route to the Application checkbox, as this service does not need to be exposed externally. Then click Create (see Figure 6-6).

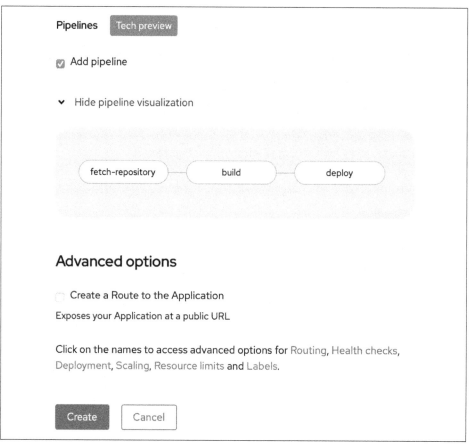

Figure 6-6. Configuring the quarkus-backend deployment's pipelines and advanced options

Inspect the Backend Resources

We can use the OpenShift CLI to inspect the backend resources. First you need to change the project you are working on to the newly created o4d-noted:

```
$ oc project o4d-noted
Now using project "o4d-noted" on server "https://api.apps-crc.testing:6443".
```

Now inspect the resources that were created. all is a useful shortcut for listing each standard OpenShift API resource that is common with deployment services, such as pod, service, route, deployment, replicaset, build, buildconfig, imagestream, job, and cronjobs:

```
$ oc get all
NAME                                     READY    STATUS …
pod/quarkus-backend-1-build             0/1      Completed
pod/quarkus-backend-5c84d4754f-5vsxp    1/1      Running

NAME                        TYPE        … PORT(S)
service/quarkus-backend     ClusterIP    8080/TCP,8443/TCP,8778/TCP

NAME                                 READY …
deployment.apps/quarkus-backend     1/1

NAME                                            DESIRED  CURRENT  READY …
replicaset.apps/quarkus-backend-5c84d4754f     1        1        1
replicaset.apps/quarkus-backend-74dcd74d86     0        0        0
```

When you are instantiating the quarkus-backend deployment, a few Kubernetes resources get created to manage the current state of the application. A replicaset is managed by the deployment resource and will keep track of and manage the desired versus available number of quarkus-backend pods that are running. A service also was created to spread the load across any other quarkus-backend components. You will see this in practice when you scale up the backend in the next chapter:

```
NAME                                                TYPE    FROM …
buildconfig.build.openshift.io/quarkus-backend Source  Git@main

NAME                        TYPE     FROM         STATUS …
Build…/quarkus-backend-1    Source   Git@c718b6b  Complete

NAME                            IMAGE REPOSITORY …
Imagestream…/quarkus-backend    …/o4d-noted/quarkus-backend
```

The output continues to show resources that are related to building the application as the pipeline resource configures native OpenShift resources to handle the build task. A buildconfig contains the configuration needed to instantiate a build for the container image from the GitHub repo. The imagestream provides the image registry location for the container image of the build.

Notice how there are no Routes listed in this output. You can verify that a Route was not created by querying the OpenShift CLI:

```
$ oc get route
No resources found in o4d-noted namespace.
```

Quite a few resources get created with the quarkus-backend deployment, but you may be wondering: where is the pipeline that created the buildconfig in the previous output?

```
$ oc get pipelines
NAME               AGE
quarkus-backend    3m53s
```

Notice that the `all` shortcut, as in `oc get all`, doesn't match custom resources, so custom resource types don't appear in a listing of "all". Custom resources are nevertheless full-fledged resources. So you can `describe` them and do other common API operation "verbs" on them. You'll learn more about generally working with API verbs, kinds, and objects, custom or otherwise, in Chapter 9. For now, `describe` the custom `quarkus-backend` pipeline custom resource to get an idea of how oc `describe` reveals object specification and status:

```
$ oc describe pipeline quarkus-backend
Name:          quarkus-backend
Namespace:     o4d-noted
Labels:        app.kubernetes.io/instance=quarkus-backend
               pipeline.openshift.io/runtime=java
               pipeline.openshift.io/type=kubernetes
Annotations:   <none>
API Version:   tekton.dev/v1beta1
Kind:          Pipeline
[…]
```

The first section of the description includes the labels, annotations, and name. These labels are commonly used to organize and group components in your application:

```
Spec:
  Params:
    Default:  quarkus-backend
    Name:     APP_NAME
    Type:     string
    Default:  https://github.com/btannous/quarkus-backend.git
    Name:     GIT_REPO
    [...]
```

The `spec` defines the parameters that are used in the pipeline. This configuration defines the default parameters, such as the Git repo and branch, for use in the instantiation of the pipeline, or `pipelinerun`:

```
Tasks:
  Name:  fetch-repository
  Params:
    Name:   url
    Value:  $(params.GIT_REPO)
    [...]
  Task Ref:
    Kind:  ClusterTask
    Name:  git-clone
  Workspaces:
    Name:       output
    Workspace:  workspace
  Name:         build
  Params:
    Name:   IMAGE
    Value:  $(params.IMAGE_NAME)
```

```
    [...]
Run After:
    fetch-repository
Task Ref:
    Kind:  ClusterTask
    Name:  s2i-java-11
    [...]
```

The Task stanza of the pipeline configuration lists all of the tasks that will be pro-cessed for this pipeline. Recall that Tasks execute in parallel unless they are config-ured to wait on each other, as shown by the Run After field in the preceding code.

Deploy the Frontend Component

Now you will deploy the frontend component of the Noted application.

In the Developer console, click +Add in the left column and choose the From Git tile. To configure the new nodejs-frontend component, enter **https://github.com/ openshift-for-developers/nodejs-frontend.git**. Click "Show advanced Git options"; for "Git reference" enter **main**, and for "Context dir" enter /. Leave the Source Secret box empty.

Under Builder, make sure Node.js is selected. Under General, in the Application box enter **noted**, and in the Name box enter **nodejs-frontend**.

Under Resources, make sure Deployment is selected. Under Pipelines, check the "Add pipeline" checkbox. And under Advanced Options, check the "Create a route to the application" checkbox, and then click the link for the Deployment advanced option (see Figure 6-7).

> The Git repository URL configured is the nodejs-frontend reposi-tory under the book's GitHub account. You are able to use this URL, instead of forking your own, as the following scenarios will not make any changes to the source code of the frontend.

Advanced Options

☑ Create a route to the application
Exposes your application at a public URL

Click on the names to access advanced options for Routing, Health Checks, Build Configuration, Deployment, Scaling, Resource Limits and Labels.

Figure 6-7. nodejs-frontend deployment Advanced Options links

Click the "Environment variables (runtime only)" link, and then enter the following for Name and Value, as shown in Figure 6-8:

```
COMPONENT_QUARKUS_BACKEND_HOST quarkus-backend
COMPONENT_QUARKUS_BACKEND_PORT 8080
```

Then click Create.

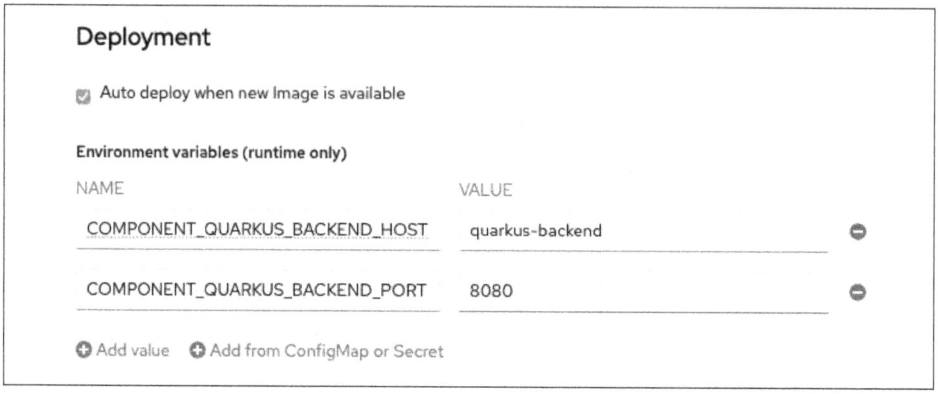

Figure 6-8. nodejs-frontend environment variable deployment configuration

In the Advanced Options of the nodejs-frontend deployment, you added two environment variables. These variables set the hostname and port of the quarkus-backend component within `src/setupProxy.js` so that the frontend knows how to retrieve the list of posts:

```
if (process.env.COMPONENT_QUARKUS_BACKEND_HOST) {
    backend_quarkus_host =
        process.env.COMPONENT_QUARKUS_BACKEND_HOST;
}

if (process.env.COMPONENT_QUARKUS_BACKEND_PORT) {
    backend_quarkus_port =
        process.env.COMPONENT_QUARKUS_BACKEND_PORT;
}
```

This hostname works, as the quarkus-backend deployment has a service that is named `quarkus-backend`. The service is accessible within the OpenShift cluster through the DNS hostname of `quarkus-backend` or the fully qualified domain name of `quarkus-backend.o4d-noted.svc.cluster.local`.

You can watch the progress of the build by clicking on Pipelines in the left sidebar, as shown in Figure 6-9. When both pipelines' *Last run status* changes to Succeeded, the components are fully built and deployed, and you can test the application! To do so, open the Route to nodejs-frontend by clicking the Open URL icon in the Topology view for the nodejs-frontend.

Figure 6-9. OpenShift Developer console pipeline status

CLI How-To: List the Pipeline Runs to See the Current Progress

List the pipeline runs in a project to inspect the current progress of the pipelines that are running using the OpenShift CLI by executing `oc get pipelineruns`.

A Running Noted Application

Welcome to the Noted web frontend, and congratulations on deploying a cloud native application! Submit at least two posts with both Title and Content. You will notice the first bug in the application: each post's title and content are displayed backward, as shown in Figure 6-10.

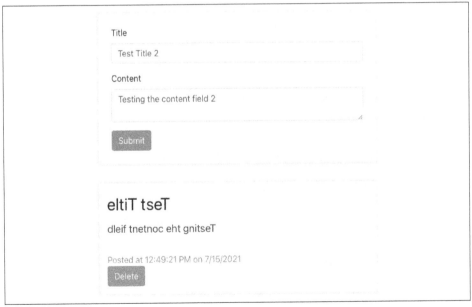

Figure 6-10. Noted application running

Automatic Pipeline Runs Using Tekton Triggers

Before you fix the display bug, it would be nice to set up some automation since you will be developing and rebuilding the quarkus-backend a few times. When you update your source code and push a commit to GitHub, a webhook or REST callback will trigger the pipeline to start and build the latest commit of your code. You need to set up a pipeline trigger to make this happen.

Pipeline Triggers

A pipeline trigger will create an EventListener pod in your project. This EventListener will also have an external URL, or route, that you can point the GitHub webhook to. This EventListener will run on OpenShift as a pod and will wait for GitHub to notify it about any source code change and act accordingly by running the corresponding pipeline.

To configure a trigger, in the Developer console, click Pipelines in the left column. Open the quarkus-backend pipeline. In the top right, click the Actions menu, and then click Add Trigger (Figure 6-11).

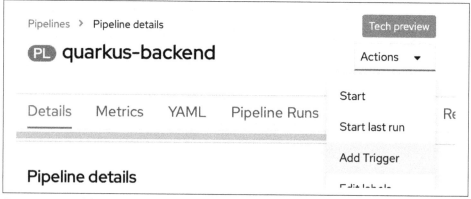

Figure 6-11. Adding a pipeline trigger for the quarkus-backend

Now you'll configure the new trigger. Under Webhook, enter **github-push** for "Git Provider type." Under Parameters, enter **quarkus-backend** for APP_Name, **https:// github.com/<your-name>/quarkus-backend.git** for GIT_REPO, and **main** for GIT_REVISION. Do not change the image_name, path_context, version, or workspace configuration. When you're finished, click Add (see Figure 6-12).

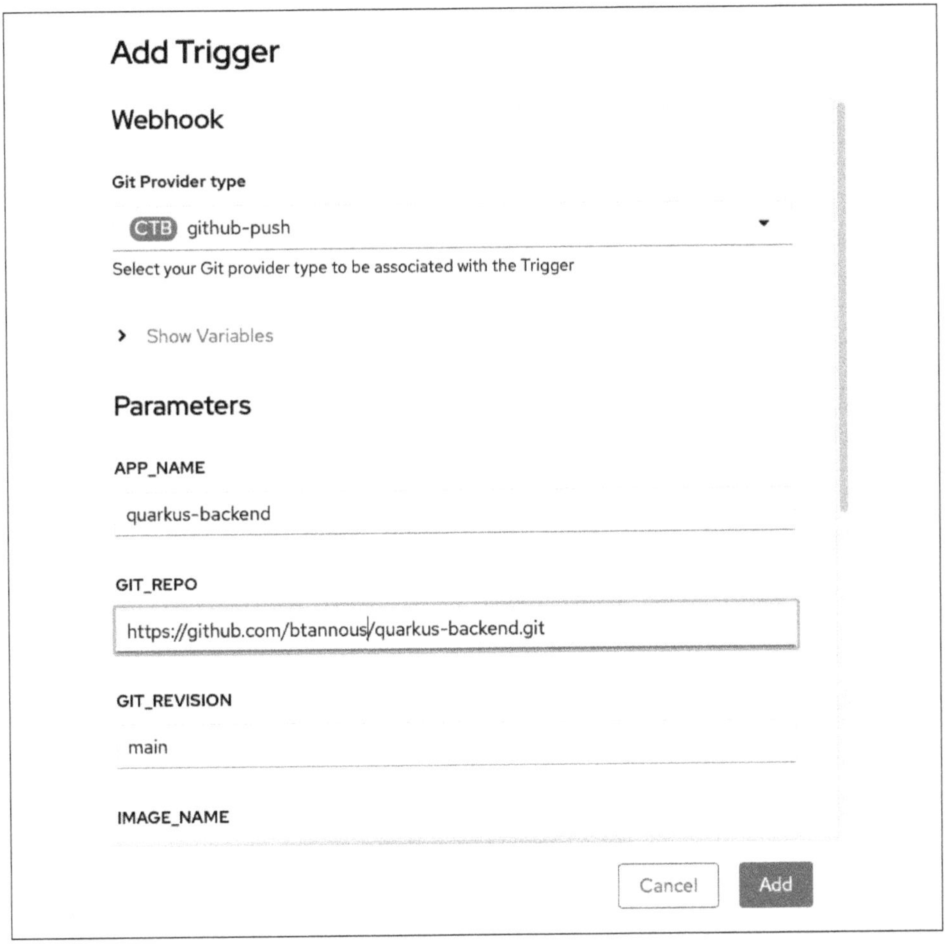

Figure 6-12. Configuring a trigger for a GitHub webhook

The Forward Proxy Workaround

One of the fundamental limitations of CodeReady Containers is that the running OpenShift cluster is isolated in a VM that is only accessible to the host computer. If you were using an OpenShift cluster that is accessible to your version control system, you would be able to use the URL of the Route for the trigger's event listener that was just created. Instead, the CRC deployment of OpenShift is local to only your workstation, and GitHub cannot send a webhook to that local-only Route. Luckily, a few forward proxy services are available for free for developers to work around this limitation. There are even a few that integrate with Kubernetes and OpenShift pretty well, such as ngrok.

The quickest way to deploy ngrok into your OpenShift CRC Deployment is to use a custom template. Templates are a way to create portable application deployments, but since we will discuss templates in Chapter 10, for now, don't worry too much about how they work.

Deploy the ngrok Template

The ngrok template requires two input variables, HOST and PORT, that you will specify to configure the forward proxy to allow ngrok to service the trigger URL:

1. First, open your terminal and make sure you are using the o4d-noted project:

```
$ oc project o4d-noted
Now using project "o4d-noted" on server
"https://api.apps-crc.testing:6443".
```

 If you do not have oc in your path, you can run crc oc-env and follow the instructions to get going.

2. To get the HOST and PORT, we will need to get the list of services and search for the name of the event-listener service to use when deploying the template in the next step:

```
$ oc get service | grep event-listener | \
    awk -F ' ' '{print $1 " PORT: " $5}'

el-event-listener-3ccb6d PORT: 8080/TCP
```

3. Deploy the ngrok template using your el-event-listener- as the HOST and be sure to configure the PORT to 8080:

```
$ oc new-app -p HOST=el-event-listener-3ccb6d -p PORT=8080 -f \
    https://raw.githubusercontent.com/openshift-for-developers/ngrok/ \
    main/ngrok.yaml

--> Deploying template "o4d-noted/ngrok" for "https://raw.githubuser..."
...
--> Success
    Access your application via route 'ngrok-o4d-noted.apps-crc.testing'
    Run 'oc status' to view your app.
```

4. Open the URL displayed in the Success output of the oc new-app command you just ran. Be sure you open this URL as HTTP:// and not HTTPS:// (Figure 6-13).

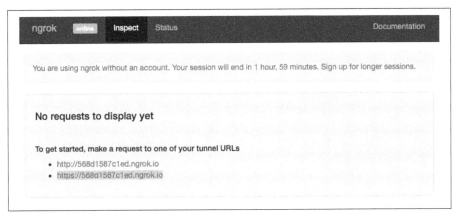

Figure 6-13. ngrok tunnel URLs

5. Next, copy the ngrok forward proxy URL, or the `https://` tunnel URL, to use for the Payload URL webhook on GitHub.

> ngrok is a free service, and the URL will only work for two hours. If you need more time, you can delete the original deployment by opening a terminal, running `oc delete all -l app=ngrok`, and redeploying the template as described in the preceding steps.

Since you are already in a terminal, try to curl the URL to validate that the ngrok forward proxy URL is deployed and working as expected:

```
$ curl https://78f8f9ea90fc.ngrok.io/

{"eventListener":"event-listener-3ccb6d","namespace":"o4d-noted",
 "errorMessage":"Invalid event body format format: unexpected end of
 JSON input"}
```

Even though your JSON response has an error, it is working as expected.

GitHub Webhook Configuration

You need to configure GitHub to notify the trigger's event listener through your ngrok forward proxy URL:

1. Open your quarkus-backend repository on GitHub and click Settings, as shown in Figure 6-14.

Figure 6-14. GitHub quarkus-backend settings

2. Select Webhooks from the left sidebar and click the "Add webhook" button, as shown in Figure 6-15.

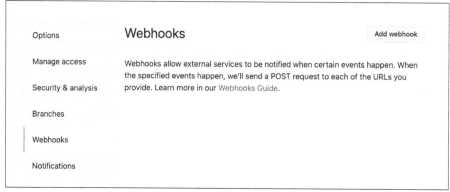

Figure 6-15. Adding a webhook in GitHub

3. Now you'll configure the webhook. For Payload URL, enter your *https://ngrok forward proxy URL*, and for "Content type," enter **application/json**. Leave the Secret box blank, as you do not need this field when using an event listener.

4. Under "SSL verification," make sure "Enable SSL verification" is selected.

5. For "Which events would you like to trigger this webhook?" make sure that "Just the push event" is selected (you only need the pipeline to rebuild when new code has been pushed to the repo).

6. Check the Active checkbox and then click "Add webhook." See Figure 6-16.

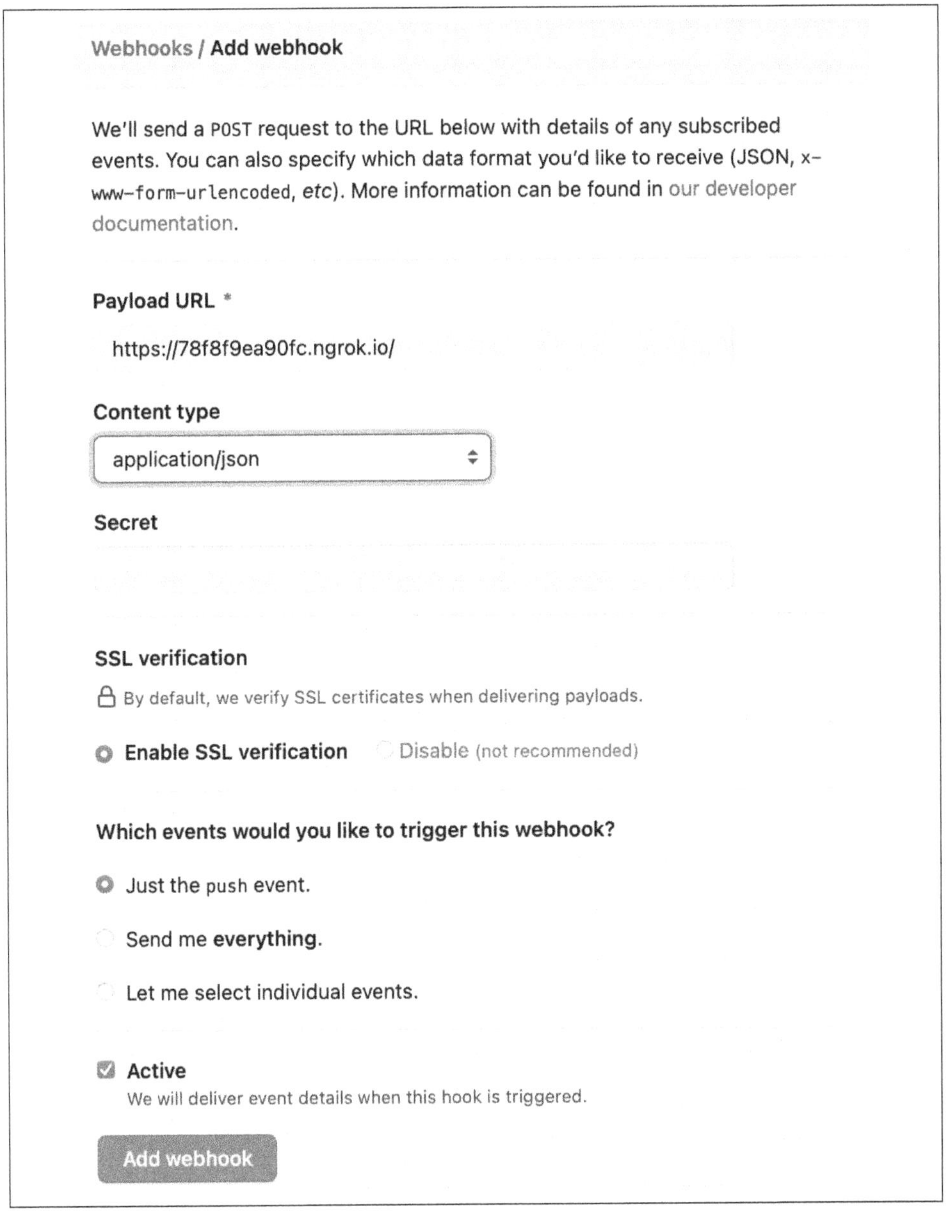

Webhooks / **Add webhook**

We'll send a POST request to the URL below with details of any subscribed events. You can also specify which data format you'd like to receive (JSON, x-www-form-urlencoded, *etc*). More information can be found in our developer documentation.

Payload URL *

https://78f8f9ea90fc.ngrok.io/

Content type

application/json ⬍

Secret

SSL verification

🔒 By default, we verify SSL certificates when delivering payloads.

🔘 **Enable SSL verification** ⚪ Disable (not recommended)

Which events would you like to trigger this webhook?

🔘 Just the push event.

⚪ Send me **everything**.

⚪ Let me select individual events.

☑ **Active**
We will deliver event details when this hook is triggered.

Add webhook

Figure 6-16. Adding a webhook in GitHub

The Reversed Text Quarkus-Backend Bug Fix

Now that your automation is configured, you can fix the title and content bug from earlier. The /posts endpoint is in the quarkus-backend *Post.java* source file.

1. First, open your quarkus-backend repository on GitHub and head to *src/main/java/com/openshift/fordevelopers/Post.java*.

   Notice that lines 26 through 32 reverse the title and content strings:

   ```
   public String getTitle() {
       return new StringBuilder(title)
         .reverse().toString();
       // Should be: return title;
   }

   public String getContent() {
       return new StringBuilder(content)
         .reverse().toString();
       // Should be: return content;
   }
   ```

   Since the issue affects only two lines of the source code, it should be quick to edit using the in-browser editor on GitHub.

2. Click the pencil icon in the upper right corner to edit the source code.

   Update the code to fix the bug, as shown in Figure 6-17.

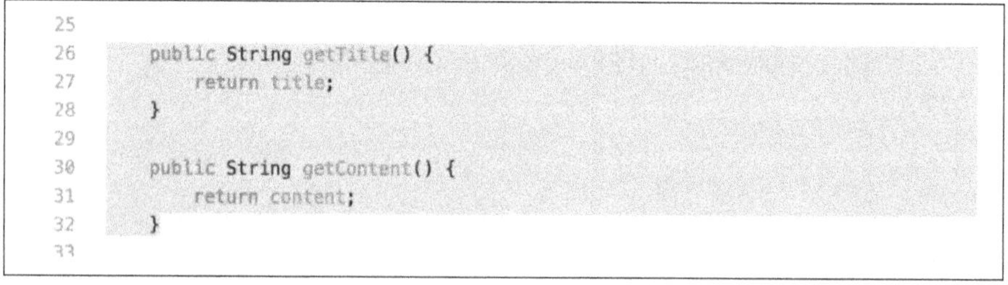

   ```
   25
   26      public String getTitle() {
   27          return title;
   28      }
   29
   30      public String getContent() {
   31          return content;
   32      }
   33
   ```

Figure 6-17. Editing Post.java on GitHub

3. Commit the fix and be sure to leave a descriptive commit message, as shown in Figure 6-18.

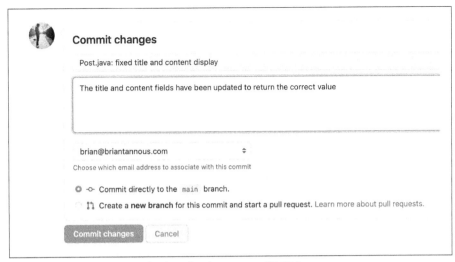

Figure 6-18. Committing the bug fix changes on GitHub

Now it's time to check out the pipeline and make sure the automation works as expected.

4. Open the OpenShift Developer console and click on Pipelines in the left sidebar.

   Notice that the quarkus-backend pipeline started automatically!

5. Click "quarkus-backend."

6. Click the Pipeline Runs tab, where you can see the status of all the pipeline runs for the quarkus-backend pipeline, as shown in Figure 6-19.

Figure 6-19. quarkus-backend pipeline runs

You can watch the output logs of the tasks in the pipeline. Compare each step's output to the tasks stanza in the quarkus-backend pipeline from "Inspect the Backend Resources" on page 50. These logs are vital for debugging within Open-Shift and should be one of the first locations you look at in the event of an error of your pipeline run.

7. Click the currently running quarkus-backend pipeline run.

8. Open the Logs tab to monitor the output of each task, as shown in Figure 6-20.

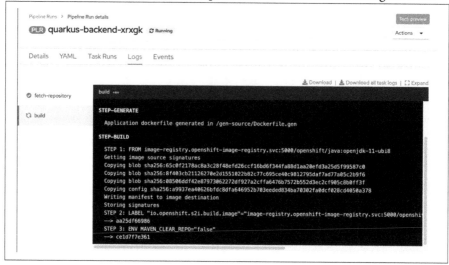

Figure 6-20. Pipeline run logs

Once the pipeline run completes, open the nodejs-frontend application route by heading to the Topology view and clicking on the Open URL icon.

Notice that the posts you added earlier have been deleted because they were stored in an in-memory array that was reset when the backend was re-created. Add that bug to the backlog to handle later.

Now, add a post or two. As shown in Figure 6-21, you should notice that the title and the content are displayed correctly!

Figure 6-21. Noted application fixed

Summary

Awesome! You deployed the nodejs-frontend and quarkus-backend components of the Noted application. You configured a webhook from GitHub, through ngrok, to your pipeline's trigger to automatically build the application after the source code had been updated on GitHub. The content display bug was also fixed and is no longer in reverse. In the next chapter, you will work with a database to save the list of posts in case of accidental restarts or deletions.

CHAPTER 7

Evolving the Application: Data Persistence

As you saw in the preceding chapter, the current deployment of the quarkus-backend only stores the list of posts in memory. Keeping lists in memory is excellent for performance, but all the posts will be lost each time the app restarts. Now, imagine if your bank lost your account information each time it decided to add a new feature or fix an issue. You'd probably be first in line at a new bank.

State is a critical aspect of many applications, and databases are one way to handle the information your application needs to keep, such as tracking your bank account's ledger or maintaining the list of notes when the quarkus-backend restarts. In this chapter, you will deploy a PostgreSQL database and bind the Noted app to it to store the posts.

Database Without Delay

If you read the subtitle of the book, you know you're supposed to be impatient. To spare you some waiting, your forked version of the quarkus-backend component already has a Git branch called pgsql with wiring in place to connect to a database. Check it out by opening a browser window to *https://github.com/<your-name>/quarkus-backend/tree/pgsql* (see Figure 7-1).

Figure 7-1. GitHub quarkus-backend pgsql branch

Database Templates

First you need to deploy a database for the pgsql branch to connect to. OpenShift makes it easy to deploy a database for development using built-in templates, as shown in Figure 7-2.

Figure 7-2. OpenShift Developer catalog database templates

However, when using a template you need to manually configure the quarkus-backend deployment to inject environment variables if you want to connect to the database. Instead, you will use the power of the OpenShift Service Binding Operators to automatically configure these environment variables.

Service Binding Operator

The Service Binding Operator (SBO) allows you to quickly bind an instance of a database to an application deployed on OpenShift without dealing with distributing secrets or configuration maps such as usernames, passwords, or connection information. The SBO can pick up a few mappings automatically, as long as the database was deployed via an operator or helm chart. The operator or helm chart will need to be developed to configure the status fields for that service as expected by the SBO.

To install the SBO, first log out of the Developer account and log back in using the administrator login provided by `crc console --credentials`.

1. Now, switch to the Administrator console.

   Open the OperatorHub via the left sidebar, search for "service binding," and choose the Service Binding Operator to install, as shown in Figure 7-3.

Figure 7-3. OperatorHub Service Binding Operator

2. Now you'll configure the installation of the SBO. For "Update channel," choose preview; for "Installation mode," choose "All namespaces on the cluster (default)"; for Installed Namespace, choose "openshift-operators"; and for "Approval strategy," choose Automatic. When you're done, click Install (see Figure 7-4).

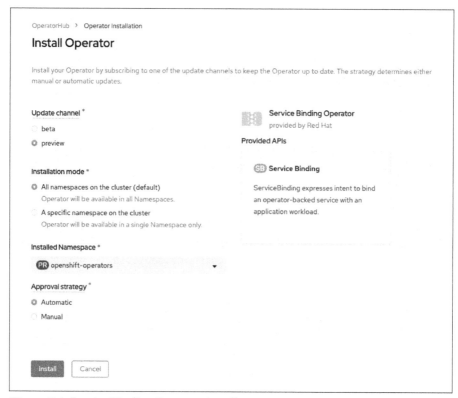

Figure 7-4. Service Binding Operator installation

The Postgres Operator Designed for Service Binding

The operator that deploys Postgres will need to be able to configure the status for each database instance as expected by the SBO. Luckily, you can use the PostgreSQL Database operator, which is used in a few examples the SBO references.

Since this operator provides the expected fields, it will be able to automatically bind configuration values for things like the username, password, database name, and other database connection info.

Add the Sample DB Operators OperatorSource

While one of the existing PostgreSQL Database operators in the OperatorHub would be able to store the list of posts, you would have to configure how the quarkus-backend connects to it manually.

Details about the Operator Lifecycle Manager are beyond the scope of this book. For more information about OLM and OperatorSources, the OLM website is a good place to start.

If you have quick and easy access to a terminal, you can run the following command to install the Postgres Database OperatorSource and then skip to "Install the PostgreSQL Database Operator" on page 72:

```
oc apply -f https://oreil.ly/hthiF
```

To set up the new PostgreSQL Database operator, you will need to install a completely new repository, or OperatorSource, that will provide the Operator Lifecycle Manager running on OpenShift with the means to install the PostgreSQL Database operator in the next step.

1. In the OpenShift console, click on the (+) icon at the top-right corner of the screen to Import YAML (see Figure 7-5).

Figure 7-5. Import YAML button

2. Add the following CatalogSource to configure a new repository for OpenShift to install operators from:

```
apiVersion: operators.coreos.com/v1alpha1
kind: CatalogSource
metadata:
    name: sample-db-operators
    namespace: openshift-marketplace
spec:
    sourceType: grpc
    image: quay.io/redhat-developer/sample-db-operators-olm:v1
    displayName: Sample DB Operators
```

OpenShift will fetch the index referenced by the CatalogSource that includes the PostgreSQL Database operator, which the new Sample DB Operators CatalogSource includes.

Install the PostgreSQL Database Operator

Wait a moment for the new CatalogSource index to be fetched. The Status will indicate READY once it's fetched, as shown in Figure 7-6.

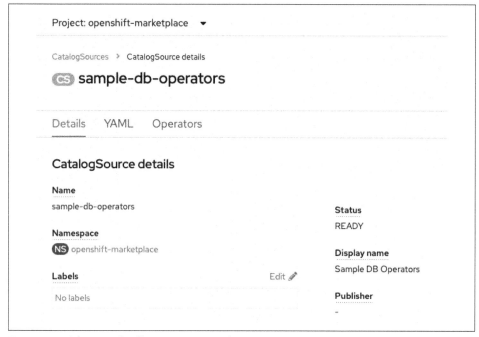

Figure 7-6. The sample-db-operators CatalogSource

Now install the PostgreSQL Database operator by opening the OperatorHub. Then follow these steps:

1. Search for PostgreSQL Database operator by clicking PostgreSQL Database, as shown in Figure 7-7.

Figure 7-7. OperatorHub PostgreSQL Database

2. Now you'll configure the installation for the PostgreSQL Database operator. Under the Install Operator, for "Update channel" choose "stable"; for "Installation

mode" choose "All namespaces on the cluster (default)"; for Installed Namespace choose "openshift-operators"; and for "Approval strategy" choose Automatic.

3. Click Install. (See Figure 7-8.)

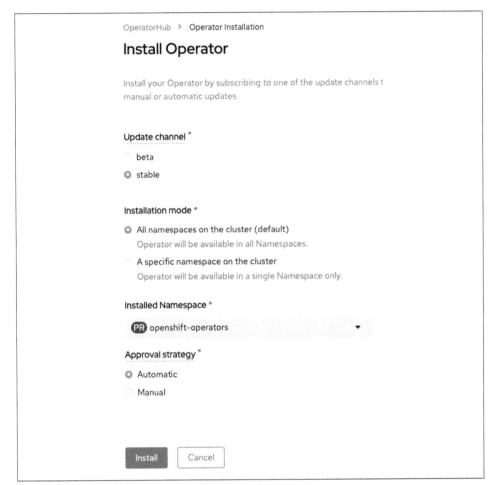

Figure 7-8. Configuring the PostgreSQL Database operator installation

Congrats! Your OpenShift cluster can now deploy a PostgreSQL Database and can automatically bind it to an application by injecting runtime environment variables into the app's deployment using the SBO.

As a developer, you may wonder how you can make this work on the application side. Don't worry! We will highlight the integration points so that you can reuse some of these ideas in your app, but first you need to deploy the database and rebuild the quarkus-backend component.

Verify Operator Installation

Now would be a good time to double-check that your OpenShift cluster has all three operators required in the next steps: the PostgreSQL Database, Red Hat OpenShift Pipelines, and Service Binding Operator.

Click Installed Operators in the left sidebar of the Administrator console to verify the operator installations, as shown in Figure 7-9.

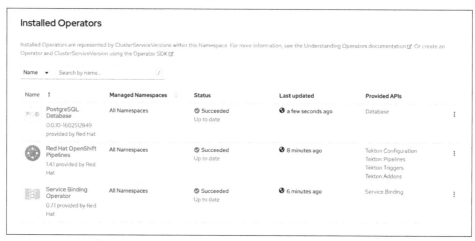

Figure 7-9. Installed operators

Deploy a PostgreSQL Database

The operators should be running smoothly.

Before you deploy the database using the newly installed operator, log out of the administrator account and login using the developer account.

Open the Developer console. Be sure you are working with the o4d-noted project. Select Add from the sidebar and then click the Database tile, as shown in Figure 7-10.

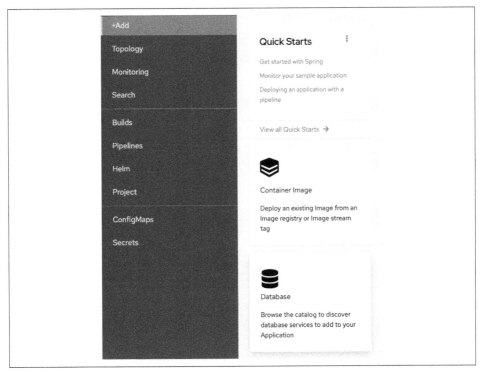

Figure 7-10. Adding a database using the Developer console

To deploy the PostgreSQL database, choose Other in the left column list of filters. Filter by the keyword Database, and then click the Operator Backed Database tile to add the PostgreSQL Database, as shown in Figure 7-11.

To accept the default installation configuration, in the Name box choose "demo-database." Leave the Labels box empty (see Figure 7-12).

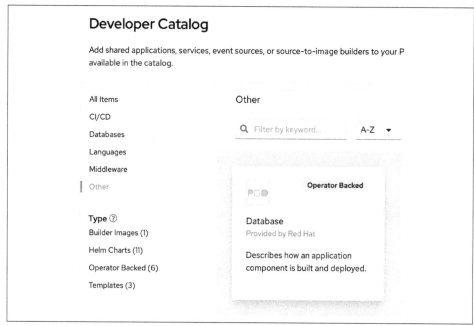

Figure 7-11. Adding the PostgreSQL Database

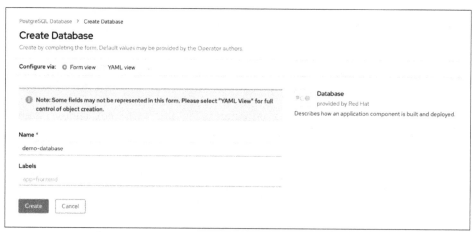

Figure 7-12. Configuring the new PostgreSQL Database

Configure the pgsql quarkus-backend Branch

Now that you have created a PostgreSQL Database, you can update the quarkus-backend to use the pgsql branch:

1. Click Pipelines in the left sidebar and Select the quarkus-backend pipeline.
2. Click on the Actions menu in the top-right corner, as shown in Figure 7-13.

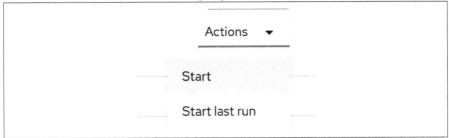

Figure 7-13. Pipeline Action Menu

3. Click Start.
4. To update the configuration of the Start Pipeline dialog, as shown in Figure 7-14, in the GIT-REVISION box enter **pgsql**.

OpenShift Pipelines will now fetch, build, and update the deployment of the pgsql branch of the quarkus-backend.

Once the pipeline has finished running, you will notice that the status of the quarkus-backend deployment will be in a CrashLoopBackOff state. This is expected, since the ServiceBinding has not been created yet and the quarkus-backend is expecting database connection configuration.

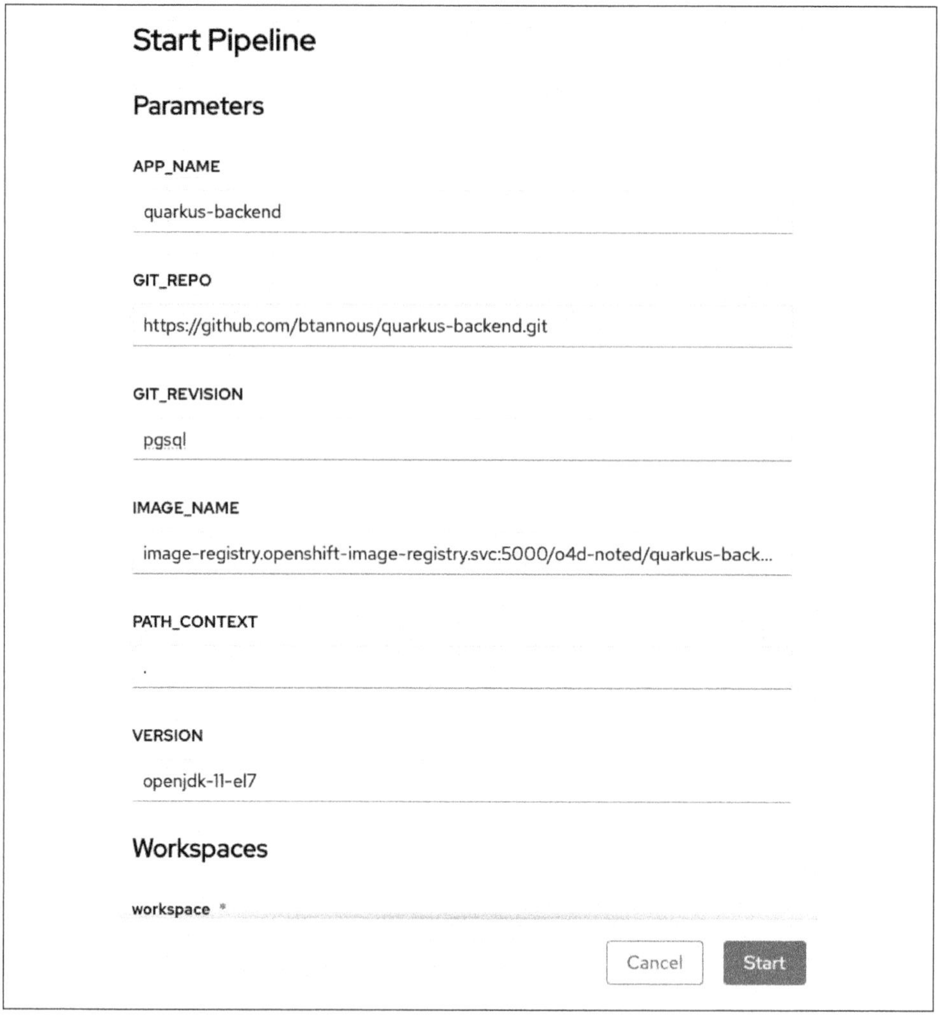

Figure 7-14. Updating the quarkus-backend pipeline to the pgsql branch

Inspect the quarkus-backend pgsql Branch

Now is an excellent time to look at the changes needed to go from in-memory to a database using quarkus by using GitHub's comparison tool.

One exciting change to be sure that you notice is how the quarkus-backend integrates with the Service Binding Operator by configuring the database connection to use the environment variables specified in the `application.properties`:

```
# quarkus-backend/src/main/resources/application.properties

# configure your datasource
quarkus.datasource.db-kind = postgresql
quarkus.datasource.username = ${DATABASE_USER:postgres}
quarkus.datasource.password = ${DATABASE_PASSWORD:password}
quarkus.datasource.jdbc.url =
  ${DATABASE_JDBC_URL:jdbc:postgresql://localhost:5432/postgres}
```

Service Binding Operator Usage

For the quarkus-backend to connect to a database, you need to configure the application.properties source file to provide details on what type of database it will connect with and how it will connect to it.

`quarkus.datasource.username` is configured with the environment variable `DATABASE_USER` value, or the default value of `postgres` if that variable is not set. Notice how the `quarkus.datasource.password` and `quarkus.datasource.jdbc.url` values are configured similarly.

This configuration allows for deployments on OpenShift using the environment variables or local development by running `mvn compile quarkus:dev` as documented in *README.md*.

By now the quarkus-backend should be redeployed, and you are able to create a `ServiceBinding` instance to automatically inject the environment variables that the `application.properties` source expects.

Using the SBO is not the only way to connect your application and database.

You can manually bind the database by configuring the quarkus-backend's Advanced Deployment option "Environment variables (runtime only)" to include the `DATABASE_USER`, `DATABASE_PASSWORD`, and `DATABASE_JDBC_URL` fields the same way you configured the nodejs-frontend in Chapter 6.

Configure a ServiceBinding

To create a service binding instance to bind the database and the quarkus-backend, you first need to open the Developer Web Console perspective.

Click the (+) icon (refer back to Figure 7-5); when you hover your cursor over the icon, a tool tip will appear that says Import YAML.

Copy each section of the YAML to import the entire ServiceBinding.

 If you happen to have quick access to a terminal, you can use the following command instead of typing out the entire ServiceBinding out:

```
oc apply -f https://raw.githubusercontent.com/
openshift-for-developers/noted/main/svc-bind-
quarkus-database.yaml
```

Next, define that this configuration is a ServiceBinding, as set by the kind configuration, and is scoped to the currently-in-use project, o4d-noted, using the the name svc-bind-quarkus-database:

```
apiVersion: binding.operators.coreos.com/v1alpha1
kind: ServiceBinding
metadata:
  name: svc-bind-quarkus-database
  namespace: o4d-noted
```

Configure the specification or spec to know which application to bind with. If the bindAsFiles value is configured as false, the ServiceBinding will inject environment variables instead of a directory of files, as shown in the SBO documentation:

```
spec:
 bindAsFiles: false
 application:
    group: apps
    name: quarkus-backend
    resource: deployments
    version: v1
```

The following services configuration defines which database to bind to the quarkus-backend. In this example, we only bind to a single database, but if you needed to bind multiple services, databases, or secrets, you could define them in this list:

```
services:
- group: postgresql.baiju.dev
  id: postgresDB
  kind: Database
  name: demo-database
  version: v1alpha1
```

The `mappings` configuration defines the custom variables to bind. The `DATA BASE_JDBC_URL` field is built here:

```
value: >
  'jdbc:postgresql://{{ .postgresDB.status.dbConnectionIP }}:
  {{ .postgresDB.status.dbConnectionPort }}/{{ .postgresDB.status.dbName }}'
```

Import the `svc-bind-quarkus-database` ServiceBinding by clicking Create.

Test the ServiceBinding

Now the database is bound, as shown in Figure 7-15 by the arrow between the quarkus-backend and demo-database in the Topology view.

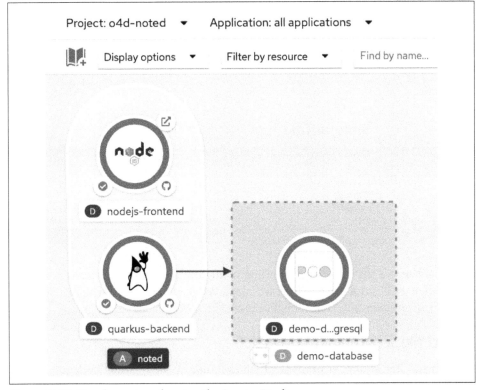

Figure 7-15. Topology view showing the ServiceBinding

Test the app. It should be fully functional!

You now should have a database that is connected with the quarkus-backend, thereby storing its posts statefully.

Open the frontend URL and notice that each post's delete button now works as well (see Figure 7-16)! Quarkus really makes working with Postgres databases simple by using Hibernate ORM with Panache as used in the quarkus-backend component.

Be sure at least one post has been added before moving on.

Figure 7-16. The stateful Noted application

You might notice that the ServiceBinding configuration did not have any *credential information*. Still, since the database was deployed using an operator that is aware of the SBO, it automatically picked up on those values—and a few more.

Inspect the ServiceBinding Injection

You can see the list of environment variables in use by the quarkus-backend deployment by opening the Topology view and clicking on the quarkus-backend icon:

1. Click on the quarkus-backend Resources link in the right sidebar, as shown in Figure 7-17.

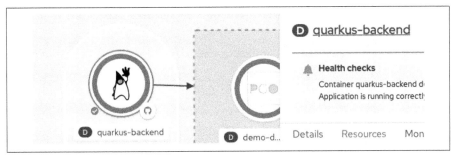

Figure 7-17. quarkus-backend Resources link

2. Open the Environment tab and look at the "All values from existing ConfigMaps or Secrets (envFrom)" field, as shown in Figure 7-18.

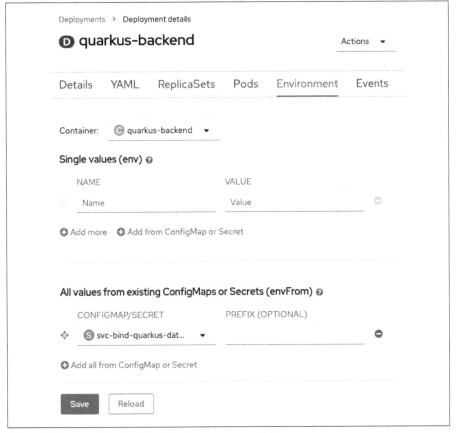

Figure 7-18. quarkus-backend environment variables

3. The SBO stores the environment variables inside a secret, as shown in Figure 7-18.

4. Search for your secret in use by first checking the Secret checkbox in the Resources dropdown.

   Now click on your "svc-bind-quarkus-database-__" secret in the list of secrets, as shown in Figure 7-19.

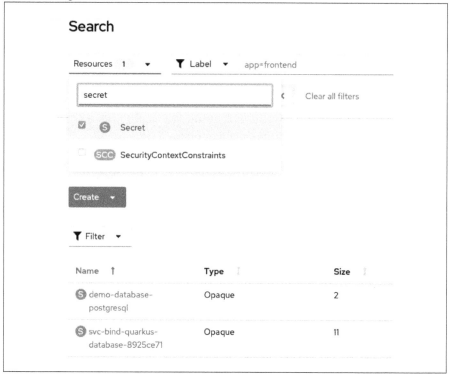

Figure 7-19. Searching for the ServiceBinding secret

5. Click the "Reveal values" link to see each configured variable that the Service-Binding creates to bind to the quarkus-backend as environment variables (Figure 7-20).

 CLI How-To: Expose the Secrets

You can use the OpenShift CLI to get all the secrets using the following command:

```
oc get secret <secret name> -o jsonpath='{.data}'
```

Note that the secret values will be base64 encoded.

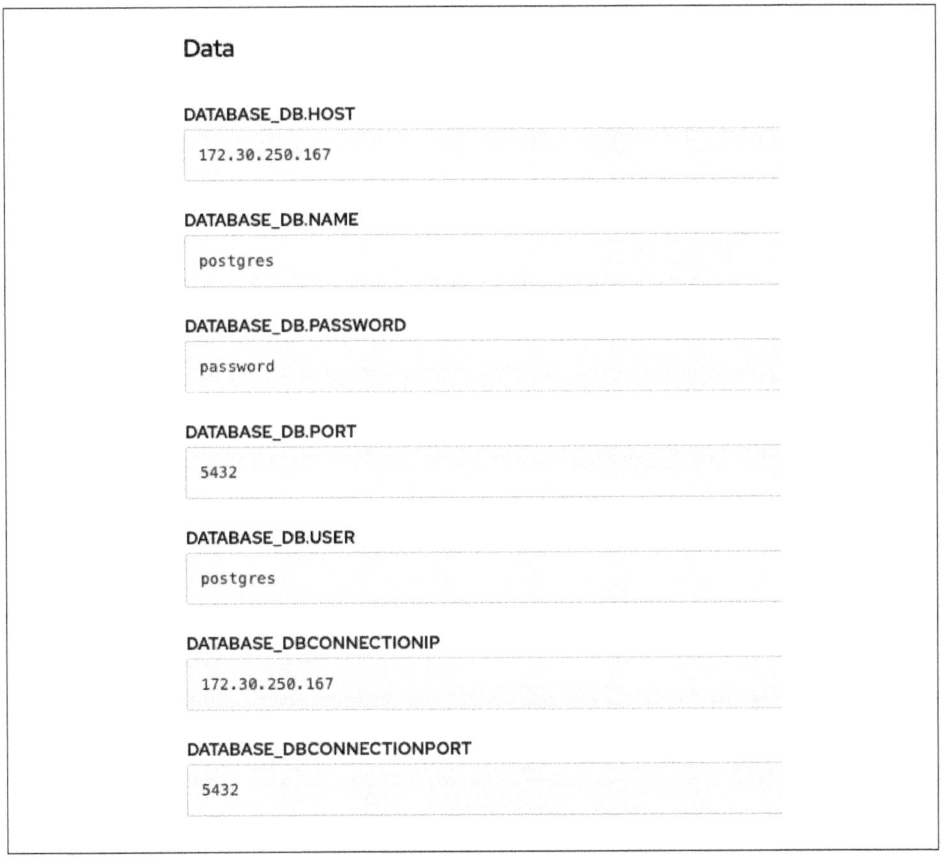

Data

DATABASE_DB.HOST

```
172.30.250.167
```

DATABASE_DB.NAME

```
postgres
```

DATABASE_DB.PASSWORD

```
password
```

DATABASE_DB.PORT

```
5432
```

DATABASE_DB.USER

```
postgres
```

DATABASE_DBCONNECTIONIP

```
172.30.250.167
```

DATABASE_DBCONNECTIONPORT

```
5432
```

Figure 7-20. The svc-bind-quarkus-database secrets revealed

You can further inspect the database to see where some of the environment variables such as `.postgresDB.status.dbConnectionIP` or `.postgresDB.status.dbName` come from to use in the ServiceBinding using the oc CLI:

```
$ oc describe database demo-database


Name:          demo-database
Namespace:     o4d-noted-pgsql
Labels:        <none>
Annotations:   <none>
API Version:   postgresql.baiju.dev/v1alpha1
Kind:          Database
...
Spec:
  Db Name:     postgres
  Image:       docker.io/postgres
  Image Name:  postgres
```

```
Status:
    Db Config Map:       demo-database
    Db Connection IP:    172.30.250.167
    Db Connection Port:  5432
    Db Credentials:      demo-database-postgresql
    Db Name:             postgres
  Events:                <none>
```

Persistence in Action

Now that you have created and deployed a database, what happens to the application if you delete all running instances of the quarkus-backend to quickly simulate an application crash or a potential node failure of a multinode cluster? We'll give you a hint: *as a user, you shouldn't notice.*

In this test, you'll delete the quarkus-backend pod to simulate an application crash because, essentially, they are handled by the ReplicaSet controller in a similar way. If a pod is not running, but at least one instance is desired, a pod will be created.

To delete the running quarkus-backend pod, open the Topology view of the Developer console.

Click the quarkus-backend deployment, select the one running pod in the sidebar, and in the Actions menu select Delete Pod, as shown in Figure 7-21.

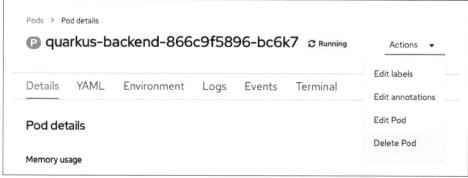

Figure 7-21. Deleting the running quarkus-backend pod

CLI How-To: Delete a Pod and Scale a Deployment

You can forcefully delete a pod by first listing the pods that are running using `oc get pods` and then running `oc delete pod <pod name>`.

Another way to redeploy the quarkus-backend deployment could be to scale it down to zero and back up to one using the following commands:

```
oc scale deployment quarkus-backend --replicas 0
oc scale deployment quarkus-backend --replicas 1
```

Now head back to the Topology view. Notice that the quarkus-backend should be running. Open the *nodejs-frontend* URL to test the Noted application.

You should notice that the posts that were posted earlier should persist after reloading the frontend URL for the Noted app.

Summary

In this chapter, you deployed the Service Binding Operator and a PostgreSQL Database operator. You used them both to enable the quarkus-frontend component to preserve the list of notes. You're ready to disrupt the social media industry with your new Noted application. So what happens when a bunch of new users show up? You'd better be ready to scale up your application with more running instances. You'll learn how to do that in the next chapter.

CHAPTER 8

Production Deployment and Scaling

Now that you have deployed the Noted application with a database, we can talk about some basic tasks that you might need to perform to make the platform work for your app. First you will need to scale the quarkus-backend component to run multiple instances and handle more load. Since a few instances of your backend component will be running, we will discuss how OpenShift can deploy updates to the fleet and potentially roll out an update to your app with zero downtime using the proper deployment strategy for your specific application. OpenShift also has robust health checking built in to make sure things are running as expected, which we'll cover in this chapter as well.

Application Scaling

OpenShift has some powerful built-in mechanisms in place that allow your application to scale by replicating. When a deployment scales upward its replica set creates additional pods for an application. The service associated with this deployment will perform the simple task of spreading the load across the replica set. The number of replicas that a deployment has can be configured manually or automatically based on CPU, memory, or concurrency metrics, as you will see and configure in the sections that follow.

Manual Scaling

Manually scaling the quarkus-backend deployment is a quick and easy way for your application to be able to handle more load.

Open the Topology view to manually scale the quarkus-backend. Select "quarkus-backend," and click the Details tab in the slideout. Then click the ∧ icon to deploy at least two quarkus-backend pods, as shown in Figure 8-1.

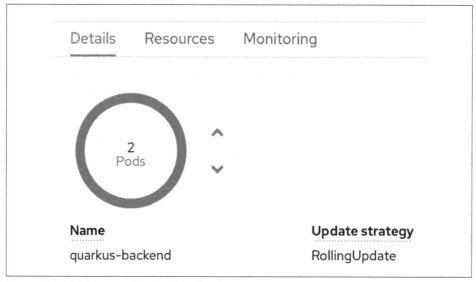

Figure 8-1. Adding quarkus-backend pods

Increasing the count adds more pods to the deployment. OpenShift will attempt to run the desired number of pods as hardware resources allow. These pods use a service to load-balance the incoming quarkus-backend API requests.

CLI How-To: Scale an Application

You can configure your application's scale using the OpenShift CLI by executing `oc scale --replicas=<desired replica count> <name>`.

The Service Abstraction

Services, introduced in Chapter 2, are a key component of how OpenShift makes scaling as simple as clicking an up arrow.

Click on the Resources tab in the quarkus-backend slideout and open the quarkus-backend service, as shown in Figure 8-2.

In Figure 8-2, you can see the details for the quarkus-backend service. This cluster-wide service has ports that are configured to be available via the cluster IP, or they can be more easily found at `service-name.project-name.svc.cluster.local` or in the case of quarkus-backend, `quarkus-backend.o4d-noted.svc.cluster.local`.

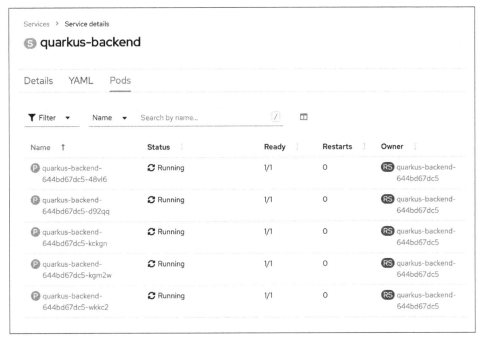

Services

⑤ quarkus-backend
Service port: **8080-tcp** ➔ Pod Port: **8080**
Service port: **8443-tcp** ➔ Pod Port: **8443**
Service port: **8778-tcp** ➔ Pod Port: **8778**

Figure 8-2. quarkus-backend services

You can see all the pods that are load-balanced across this service by opening the Pods tab (see Figure 8-3).

Services > Service details

⑤ **quarkus-backend**

Details   YAML   Pods

▼ Filter ▾   Name ▾   Search by name...

Name ↑	Status	Ready	Restarts	Owner
ⓟ quarkus-backend-644bd67dc5-48vl6	↻ Running	1/1	0	ⓡⓢ quarkus-backend-644bd67dc5
ⓟ quarkus-backend-644bd67dc5-d92qq	↻ Running	1/1	0	ⓡⓢ quarkus-backend-644bd67dc5
ⓟ quarkus-backend-644bd67dc5-kckgn	↻ Running	1/1	0	ⓡⓢ quarkus-backend-644bd67dc5
ⓟ quarkus-backend-644bd67dc5-kgm2w	↻ Running	1/1	0	ⓡⓢ quarkus-backend-644bd67dc5
ⓟ quarkus-backend-644bd67dc5-wkkc2	↻ Running	1/1	0	ⓡⓢ quarkus-backend-644bd67dc5

Figure 8-3. quarkus-backend service's pods

You may be wondering: how does the quarkus-backend service select the pods to be load-balanced?

Well, let's see by inspecting the quarkus-backend service. Click on the YAML tab. The service matches the pods that are labeled with the same configuration under the `.spec.selector` stanza within the service:

```
kind: Service
apiVersion: v1
metadata:
  name: quarkus-backend
  [...]
spec:
  selector:
    app: quarkus-backend
    deploymentconfig: quarkus-backend
  [...]
```

Here you can compare the selector with how the quarkus-backend deployment has been labeled.

Open the quarkus-backend deployment by heading to the Toplogy view. Click on the quarkus-backend icon, and then open the Details tab on the slideout.

Notice how the deployment has a label that matches the service's `app: quarkus-backend` selector, as shown in Figure 8-4.

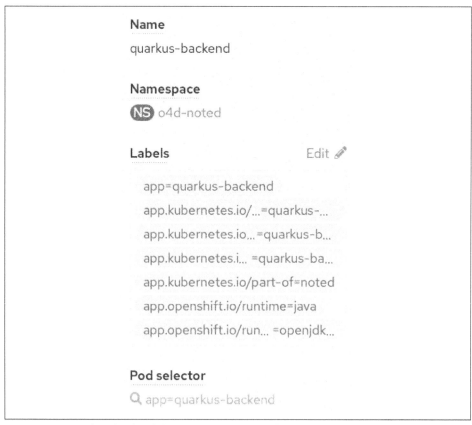

Figure 8-4. quarkus-backend deployment labels and selector

CLI How-To: Working with Services and Selectors

You can list the services in your cluster using the OpenShift CLI command `oc get service`.

You can also list the endpoints that match to pods that are load-balanced across a particular service by running these commands:

```
oc describe service <service name>
```

```
oc get service <service name> -o yaml
```

You can list all the pods that match a specific label or selector using the OpenShift CLI command `oc get pods -l <label=value>`.

Automatic Scaling

Scaling an application by clicking an up or down arrow is awesome and makes it so that you can quickly define how many replicas are available to your application. This allows you to manually grow your application to be able to handle more users. However, in most cases automated scaling is preferred in production environments as it will allow you to maximize the available resources to your application by reacting to its usage.

The Horizontal Pod Autoscaler

The Horizontal Pod Autoscaler (HPA) is one of the automatic scaling mechanisms built into OpenShift that will automatically scale your application deployment based on a CPU and memory threshold that you define. These metrics are captured using Prometheus, an open source monitoring solution that is included with the OpenShift Container Platform. You will explore Prometheus and OpenShift monitoring in Chapter 9.

Prometheus is disabled using CRC as it would require additional resources in a potentially already constrained workstation. You will configure the quarkus-backend to scale using an HPA, but due to this limitation, the actual automated scaling will not work.

To configure an HPA, you need a deployment that specifies memory as well as CPU requests and limits so that the HPA knows what to base the load threshold on. Therefore, you will need to edit the quarkus-backend deployment to add these metrics, as they were not configured in the deployment step in Chapter 6.

Update the quarkus-backend requests and limits

Requests and limits can be added at creation of a deployment or updated after an application has been deployed, as in the case of quarkus-backend. These simple configuration specifications define the minimum and maximum CPU and memory that deployments are allowed to consume. It is *always* recommended to configure requests and limits for *every deployment* on OpenShift. An application could clobber 100% of the CPU of the entire cluster at the expense of every other running workload on that individual node without the guardrails that limits and requests provide.

You can edit the configuration to add the requests and limits and then rebind it back to the database:

1. Open the Topology view. Select the quarkus-backend deployment, and in the Actions menu in the upper-right corner, select "Edit quarkus-backend," as shown in Figure 8-5.

Figure 8-5. Editing in the quarkus-backend Actions menu

2. In the "Advanced options" configuration, click on the "Resource limits" link, as shown in Figure 8-6.

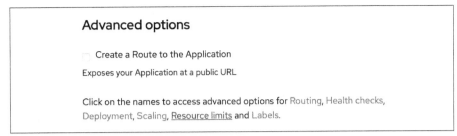

Figure 8-6. "Resource limits" link

3. Configure the Resource limit. For CPU Request choose "100 millicores"; for CPU Limit choose "1 cores"; for Memory Request choose "250 Mi"; and for Memory Limit choose "500 Mi." When you're finished, click Save. (See Figure 8-7.)

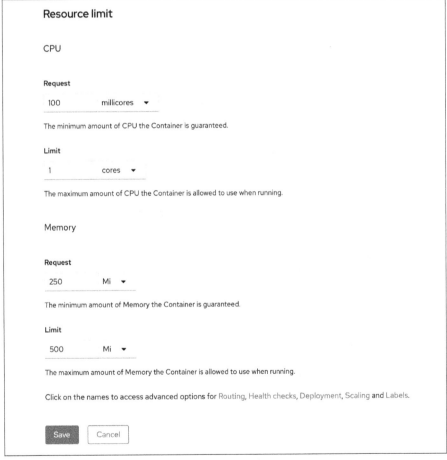

Figure 8-7. quarkus-backend resource limits and requests

Rest assured, now the quarkus-backend will not be able to overrun the available resources for your OpenShift cluster due to the configured limits.

Configure a Horizontal Pod Autoscaler

The quarkus-backend now has CPU and memory limits and requests, so you are able to configure the Horizontal Pod Autoscaler to autoscale based on the load:

1. Open the Developer console's Topology view. Click on the quarkus-backend deployment icon, and in the Actions menu, click Add HorizontalPodAutoscaler, as shown in Figure 8-8.

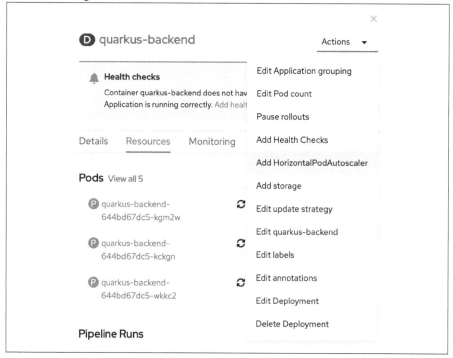

Figure 8-8. Adding an HPA for the quarkus-backend deployment

2. To configure the HorizontalPodAutoscaler, for Name choose "hpa-quarkus-backend"; for Minimum Pods choose "1"; for Maximum Pods choose "5"; for CPU Utilization choose "80%"; and for Memory Utilization choose "80%." When you're finished, click Save. (See Figure 8-9.)

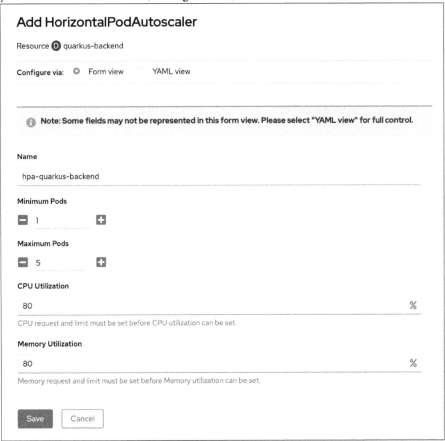

Figure 8-9. Configuring the hpa-quarkus-backend

Now the quarkus-backend is configured to autoscale once 80% of its CPU or memory limit has been consumed.

Verify autoscaling

Open the Details tab for the quarkus-backend in the Topology view. You will see the Pod Count displayed as *Autoscaled to ...*, indicating that OpenShift is automatically scaling this service (see Figure 8-10).

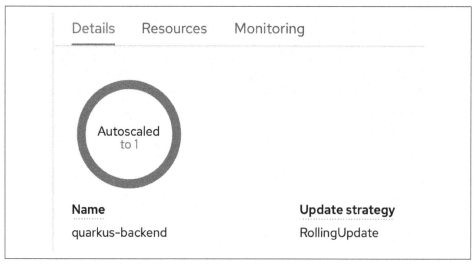

Figure 8-10. quarkus-backend autoscaled

Your deployment might be autoscaled to a different value than displayed in Figure 8-10 due to the manual scaling exercise and Prometheus not being enabled.

The quarkus-backend is now configured to automatically scale based on the load. You even configured limits to not allow it to grow out of control and take over all of the cluster resources.

Health Checks

Now that you don't need to focus on manually scaling your Noted application components, you can rest easy knowing that it will always be available. What happens if the quarkus-backend is up and running in a noncrashed state but is not processing things as expected?

At the moment: *nothing at all.*

OpenShift's health-checking functionality can automatically poll your application using HTTP, TCP, or container commands to verify that it is healthy. The poll's response will be compared to a preconfigured expected value. OpenShift can attempt to redeploy a deployment with a failed health check as well as notify administrators about the health issue.

The quarkus-backend has a basic implementation of the quarkus extension SmallRye Health (*https://oreil.ly/vfeCR*) that is configured with a few health-checking probe endpoints defined in the following sections.

Health-Checking Probes

Health-checking probes provide the polling functionality to guarantee that your application is up, healthy, and responding as expected. There are three common health checks that you can configure when deploying your application on OpenShift: Readiness, Liveness, and Startup.

Readiness probe

A readiness probe determines whether a container is ready to accept service requests. If the readiness probe fails for a container, it will be removed from the list of available service endpoints. After a failure, the probe continues to poll the pod. If it becomes available, OpenShift will add the pod to the list of available service endpoints.

The quarkus-backend is configured to respond to the readiness probe based on its Postgres connection status at the endpoint /health/ready.

We use a remote shell, as we explain in Chapter 9, to show you the output of this endpoint so that you can configure OpenShift's health-checking functionality in the next section:

```
$ curl quarkus-backend.o4d-noted.svc.cluster.local:8080/health/ready

{
    "status": "UP",
    "checks": [
        {
            "name": "Database connections health check",
            "status": "UP"
        }
    ]
}
```

Liveness probe

A liveness probe determines whether a container is still running. The container will be killed if the liveness probe fails due to a condition such as a deadlock. The pod then responds based on its restart policy.

The quarkus-backend's /health/live endpoint is configured to respond with the liveness of the application:

```
sh-4.4$ curl quarkus-backend:8080/health/live

{
    "status": "UP",
    "checks": [
    ]
}
```

Startup probe

A startup probe indicates whether the application within a container is started. All other probes are disabled until the startup succeeds. If the startup probe does not succeed within a specified period, OpenShift will kill the container, usually restarting it immediately after.

Configure the Health Checks in OpenShift

Now you are able to configure the health checking within OpenShift. This will instruct the cluster to begin polling the health endpoints of the quarkus-backend to verify that it is healthy and ready to process posts:

1. First, open the OpenShift Developer console's Topology view. Then click on the quarkus-backend deployment, and in the Actions menu, click Add Health Checks.

2. We will configure only the liveness and readiness probes for the quarkus-backend. To do so, configure the health checks as follows. Start by adding a readiness probe by choosing HTTP GET in the Type field. Under HTTP Headers, for the Path enter **/health/ready** and for the Port enter **8080**.

   Next, you will choose a series of thresholds:

   Failure threshold: 3
   > The failure threshold is how many times the probe will try starting or restarting before giving up.

   Success threshold: 1
   > The success threshold is how many consecutive successes are required for the probe to be considered successful after having failed.

   Initial delay: 30 seconds
   > The initial delay is how long to wait after the container starts before checking its health.

   Period: 10 seconds
   > The period is how often to perform the probe

   Timeout: 1 second
   > The timeout is how long to wait for the probe to finish. If the time is exceeded, the probe will be considered a failure.

3. Make your threshold selections. For Failure choose "3"; for Success choose "1"; for "Initial delay" choose "30 seconds"; for Period choose "10 seconds"; and for Timeout choose "1 second." See Figure 8-11.

Edit health checks Learn more 🗗

Health checks for Ⓓ quarkus-backend

Container ⓒ quarkus-backend

Readiness probe Edit Probe

A readiness probe checks if the Container is ready to handle requests. A failed readiness probe means that a Container should not receive any traffic from a proxy, even if it's running.

Type

HTTP GET   ▾

☐ Use HTTPS

HTTP Headers

HEADER NAME   VALUE

Header name   Value   ☺

⊕ Add header

Path

/health/ready

Figure 8-11. Configuring the quarkus-backend readiness probe

4. Click the check mark, as shown in Figure 8-12, to save the probe.

Figure 8-12. Saving the probe by clicking the check mark button

5. To configure the liveness probe, choose HTTP GET in the Type field. Under HTTP Headers, for the Path enter **/health/live** and for the Port enter **8080**.

6. For the Failure threshold choose "3"; for the Success threshold choose "1"; for "Initial delay" choose "30 seconds"; for Period choose "10 seconds"; and for Timeout choose "1 second."

7. Click the check mark button.

8. Click Save to save the updated deployment.

OpenShift can now programmatically detect whether the deployment is ready and working based on the health checks built into the quarkus-backend component. This offloads certain failure states that the health-check probes monitor to attempt to be automatically redeployed, resulting in fewer manual tasks for teams running production systems.

Production Deployment Strategies

A few different types of production deployment strategies are available within OpenShift that allow you to determine how OpenShift handles rolling out your application in the event of an update, creation, updated scale, or if a pod was killed for some other reason.

Available Deployment Strategies on OpenShift

This section details the available strategies, as well as how the strategy that is used is determined by the constraints of the specific application.

Rolling deployment strategy

A rolling deployment is the default and most common deployment strategy within OpenShift. This method slowly replaces instances of the previous version of an application with instances of the new version of the application. If your deployment has heath checking configured, a rolling deployment will wait for new pods to become ready via a readiness check before scaling down the old components.

Rolling deployments are used when you would like updates with no downtime. One requirement of rolling deployments is that your application needs to support having old code and new code running at the same time. Typically, this requirement is not an issue in general deployments.

Canary deployments

A canary deployment is a common deployment paradigm that tests a new version of an application before rolling it out to the entire install base of that app. In fact, in OpenShift, all rolling deployments are canary deployments. The canary version, or the new version in a deployment update, is tested before all the old instances of that deployment are replaced. If the canary crashes immediately or if a configured readiness check never succeeds, the canary will be removed and the deployment will be automatically rolled back to the previously known working deployment.

Recreate deployment strategy

The recreate strategy has basic rollout behavior and could be used when your application is not able to run alongside an older version. This method will completely scale the deployment down to zero and then scale the deployment back up using the new version of your application. Be aware that using the recreate deployment strategy will incur downtime during updates as the deployment will scale down to zero for a brief period.

Recreate deployment strategies can also be used during one-time migrations or other data transformations before your new version starts; just switch the strategy for the update. Recreate deployments also need to be used when you want your deployment to use a persistent volume with strict writing requirements that specify that only one pod can mount the volume at a time. To put it another way, recreate deployments need to be used when the deployment needs to be configured to mount the volume with the access mode of read-write-once.

Custom deployment strategy

Custom deployments are...custom! You can customize how your deployment rolls out on OpenShift if the application has specific needs. This type of deployment strategy allows you to run custom commands for each rollout, and you are able to base your deployment rollout on the specific needs of a given application as well.

See the OpenShift documentation (*https://oreil.ly/DYGoB*) for more information on how to customize deployments for your app's requirements.

Are There Servers in Serverless?

Of course! Sometimes those servers run OpenShift.

While discussing Serverless in detail is beyond the scope of this book, we suggest you check out the serverless model for your applications. It abstracts even more of the systems management required to develop and deploy applications. OpenShift Serverless is powered by the open source Knative project, and it provides an automated and opinionated way to deploy and scale applications and functions in response to events.

An event-driven serverless deployment, for example, makes it possible to run code and provision infrastructure only when necessary. That allows the application to be idle when it isn't needed. A serverless application will automatically scale up based on event triggers in response to incoming demand, and it can scale down to zero afterward.

To learn more about OpenShift Serverless and Knative, check out *Knative Cookbook: Building Effective Serverless Applications with Kubernetes and OpenShift* by Burr Sutter and Kamesh Sampath (O'Reilly).

Configuring a Deployment Strategy

You can easily configure rolling or recreate deployment strategies using the Developer console.

Open the Developer console Topology view. Select "quarkus-backend," and in the Actions menu, click Edit Update Strategy. Notice how to change the strategy, and then click Cancel, as shown in Figure 8-13.

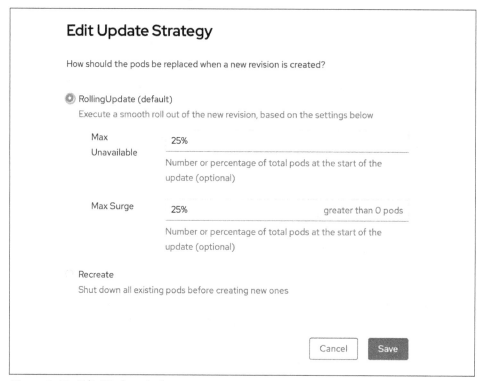

Figure 8-13. Edit Update deployment strategy

Deployment Rollbacks

OpenShift makes it easy to roll back a deployment if something doesn't work correctly with your rolled-out version. You can use the OpenShift command line to determine the rollout history for a specific deployment and then perform the rollback, as shown here (the latest revision will be at the end of the rollout history list):

```
$ oc rollout history deployment/quarkus-backend
deployment.apps/quarkus-backend
REVISION  CHANGE-CAUSE
1         <none>
2         <none>
3         <none>
```

```
$ oc rollout undo deployment/quarkus-backend --to-revision=<Revision Number>
deployment.apps/quarkus-backend rolled back
```

While your revision numbers may differ, you can validate that the quarkus-backend
has been rolled back by listing the history again:

```
% oc rollout history deployment/quarkus-backend
deployment.apps/quarkus-backend
REVISION   CHANGE-CAUSE
1          <none>
3          <none>
2          <none>
```

Summary

In this chapter, you learned how to manually scale the Noted app's backend component, as you might do when you're testing and measuring an application to determine
its baseline number of replicas and resources. Then you configured OpenShift to
automatically scale to more or fewer quarkus-backends in response to demand. You
also did the important job of configuring a health check for the quarkus-backend. In
the next chapter, you'll learn more about OpenShift's metrics and monitoring tools
and views.

CHAPTER 9

Monitoring and Managing Applications on OpenShift

You've made an application with multiple components, and you've automated its build and deployment with a repeatable pipeline. You've set up OpenShift to watch your applications and take action on your behalf when they need to be scaled in response to demand or restarted in response to their going sideways. You're in a good position to focus on your application's features and code, because when everything goes right, you commit changes and OpenShift handles the rest.

But no one defies Murphy's Law forever. Eventually you'll need to troubleshoot your application, or its deployment, by examining its moving parts, available cluster resources, and the logs that record build, deployment, and application events. This chapter introduces the most common OpenShift tools for examining running resources, from listing them to check their basic status, to walking in your application's shoes by connecting to it and interactively running commands inside its container.

Listing and Detailing Resources

The `oc` tool is the simplest form of monitoring OpenShift resources. There is a general pattern for addressing a resource in an `oc` command line. You specify the action you want to do, the kind of object you want to do it to, and the name of that specific object: `oc <verb> <kind> <name>`. Specifying a kind but not a name refers to all the objects of that kind.

For example, to list all the objects of the Pod type running in the current project, use the get verb aimed at objects of the pod kind:

```
$ oc get pods
NAME                                    READY   STATUS   RESTARTS
Demo-database-postgresql-6bbdc7b9d-btn2h 1/1    Running 0
el-event-listener-4dtv4l-844ddcb4-5697h 1/1    Running 0
nodejs-frontend-5d4f95bd9d-9998w         1/1    Running 0
...
```

Notice how each instance of a running pod is suffixed with a unique ID to distinguish among replicas in a horizontally scaled deployment. Running oc get pods immediately after completing Chapter 8's exercises will print a list that includes several build pods, named with -build suffixes, and with their status marked as Completed, along with the Running pods of the Noted application's components shown here.

This is the same set of resources you'd see in the Web Console's Topology view but presented as a textual list. It is very similar to what you'll see if you switch the Topology view to list mode with the button at the top right in the Topology view, as shown in Figure 9-1.

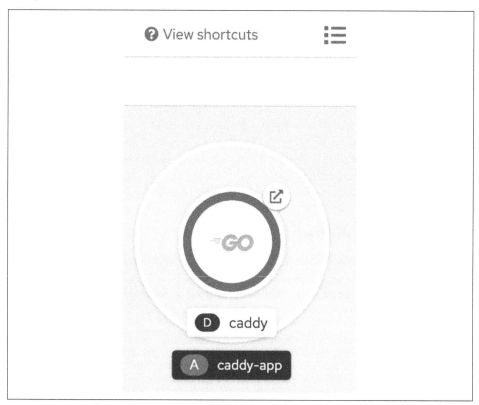

Figure 9-1. Topology view list mode toggle icon

Taking a single pod's name from the list of all pods shows how you can narrow down an API verb's target from an entire class of objects to a specific object of that type:

```
$ oc get pod nodejs-frontend-5d4f95bd9d-9998w

NAME                               READY  STATUS   RESTARTS
Nodejs-frontend-5d4f95bd9d-9998w   1/1    Running  0
```

Using Labels to Filter Listed Resources

Labels identify characteristics of API resources. The Noted application's components, for instance, are labeled with a key value pair that indicates their app is noted. You can select only those resources with a given label by passing a --selector argument to oc get naming the label and value you want. This provides a mechanism for organizing more than one application in a single Project. For example, try getting pods in your Noted application, labeled with app=noted-app:

```
$ oc get pods --selector app=noted-app
```

Describing Resources

You can learn a lot about any resource with the describe subcommand. For example, the Operators we've used to provision databases in the Noted application define their own new custom resources. Custom resources represent the things an Operator manages.

Consider how you looked for pipelines and pipelineruns to confirm progress throughout Chapter 6. Pipelines are not native Kubernetes resources. In fact, they didn't exist as a resource type on your OpenShift cluster until you bolted on the Pipelines Operator. Once the Operator was added, though, your cluster's API had new custom resource types, among them pipeline and pipelinerun. Your pipeline for building the Noted app comprised instances of those custom resources. Custom resources can be treated like any other resource in the API. For example, list all of them in a project with the get verb and the kind of object:

```
$ oc get pipelines
NAME             AGE
quarkus-backend  3m53s
```

Events and Logs

When a problem comes up, the log files are often the first troubleshooting step. You can retrieve logs for a resource with the logs verb. You'll need to drill down to a specific instance of the deployment, pod, or container whose logs you want to read. In the following excerpt, first the list of all pods is retrieved, giving the name of the single pod whose logs you want:

```
$ oc get pods
NAME                                      READY  STATUS   RESTARTS
caddy-5bf94cc5b6-qfhh2                    1/1    Running  0
El-event-listener-4dtv4l-844ddcb4-5697h   1/1    Running  0
Nodejs-frontend-5d4f95bd9d-9998w          1/1    Running  0

$ oc logs caddy-5bf94cc5b6-qfhh2
Activating privacy features... done.

Serving HTTP on port 8080
http://0.0.0.0:8080
```

Given the name of the single `caddy` pod, `logs` prints the pod's logs on standard output.

Debugging an Application in Its Container

When the problem isn't with configuration or deployment, troubleshooting moves to the application level. OpenShift's command-line tool `oc` has a set of subcommands for running things inside your application's container. You encountered one of them, `oc rsh`, back in Chapter 8. The other two are `exec` and `debug`.

oc rsh

The `rsh` subcommand takes the name of a Deployment, ReplicaSet, Pod or other running resource and sets up a connection to an interactive shell running there. By default, `rsh` picks the first container in the pod. You can specify another container in the pod by passing its name to `rsh`'s `-c` argument. The container image must include an interactive shell.

In the following excerpt, the `oc new-app` command creates a new Apache HTTP server deployment from the template included with OpenShift. Once it's running, `oc get` retrieves the name of the pod instance to pass to `oc rsh`. The `rsh` subcommand connects to the shell in the Apache container. Once connected, you can run commands inside the container to list the processes running in it, check environment variables, and generally see the world from the application's point of view:

```
$ oc new-app httpd-example
--> Deploying template "openshift/httpd-example" to project default

   Apache HTTP Server
   ---------
[...]

$ oc get pods
NAME                   READY  STATUS     RESTARTS
httpd-example-1-build  0/1    Completed  0
httpd-example-1-deploy 0/1    Completed  0
```

```
httpd-example-1-t7lhk     1/1     Running    0

$ oc rsh httpd-example-1-t7lhk  # This command drops into the container's shell

sh-4.4$ ps ax
  PID TTY    STAT   TIME COMMAND
    1 ?      Ss   0:00 httpd -D FOREGROUND
   34 ?      S    0:00 /usr/bin/coreutils --coreutils-prog-shebang=cat /usr/bin/cat
   35 ?      S    0:00 /usr/bin/coreutils --coreutils-prog-shebang=cat /usr/bin/cat
   36 ?      S    0:00 /usr/bin/coreutils --coreutils-prog-shebang=cat /usr/bin/cat
   37 ?      S    0:00 /usr/bin/coreutils --coreutils-prog-shebang=cat /usr/bin/cat
   38 ?      S    0:00 httpd -D FOREGROUND
   39 ?      Sl   0:00 httpd -D FOREGROUND
   43 ?      Sl   0:00 httpd -D FOREGROUND
   47 ?      Sl   0:00 httpd -D FOREGROUND
  253 pts/0   Ss   0:00 /bin/sh
  263 pts/0   R+   0:00 ps ax

sh-4.4$ env
HTTPD_CONTAINER_SCRIPTS_PATH=/usr/share/container-scripts/httpd/
HTTPD_DATA_ORIG_PATH=/var/www
HTTPD_EXAMPLE_PORT_8080_TCP_ADDR=10.217.4.209
SUMMARY=Platform for running Apache httpd 2.4 or building httpd-based application
HTTPD_DATA_PATH=/var/www
HOSTNAME=httpd-example-1-t7lhk
```

oc exec

The oc exec subcommand runs a specified command inside the specified container. You can exec where you can't rsh; exec can directly invoke an executable without needing a shell. For example, the caddy image in this chapter's examples doesn't include any shell, or any other executable besides the caddy web server. Nevertheless, exec can execute /bin/caddy and arrange to print its output. Like rsh, exec connects to the pod's first container by default, or to the container named in a -c argument. Unlike rsh, exec expects the target command name or executable path to be explicitly named:

```
$ oc get pods
NAME                      READY   STATUS    RESTARTS
Caddy-5bf94cc5b6-qfhh2    1/1     Running   0

$ oc rsh caddy-5bf94cc5b6-qfhh2
ERRO[0000] exec failed: container_linux.go:366: starting container process
caused: exec: "/bin/sh": stat /bin/sh: no such file or directory
command terminated with exit code 1

$ oc exec caddy-5bf94cc5b6-qfhh2 -- /bin/caddy --version
v1.11
```

oc debug

Like `rsh`, `debug` connects you to a terminal running inside a specified container that must have a shell on its PATH. Unlike `rsh` or `exec`, `debug` starts a new instance running a command shell instead of the entry point specified in the container image. Imagine a container that's failing to start with its usual server command. Run `debug` on the failing container's deployment or pod to run a new instance and bypass the failing server in favor of a shell. From the shell you can invoke the failing service by hand.

You can sometimes resuscitate a pod from a `CrashLoopBackOff` with `debug`. Because `debug` starts a new instance of the container with an entry point you specify, you can enter a shell within the container and manually trigger and step through your application's startup sequence:

```
$ oc debug deployment/hello
Starting pod/hello-debug ...
Pod IP: 10.128.2.27
If you don't see a command prompt, try pressing enter.

sh-4.2$
```

In the preceding shell excerpt, we started a new instance of the `hello` application from Chapter 4. Instead of starting the application, however, `debug` has started and wired your terminal up to a shell inside the new `hello-debug` container. From here, you can execute the `hello` binary by hand and watch it for failures as well as review the environment, network connectivity, and other application resources from the application's containerized point of view.

OpenShift Monitoring

OpenShift monitoring is built atop the open source Prometheus project. It includes monitoring for the cluster's resources, such as nodes and their CPU and memory resources, control plane pods, and platform services. It includes a set of alerts to notify cluster administrators about exceptional conditions. Dashboards in the OpenShift Web Console display graphs representing capacity and consumption across the entire cluster; see Figure 9-2.

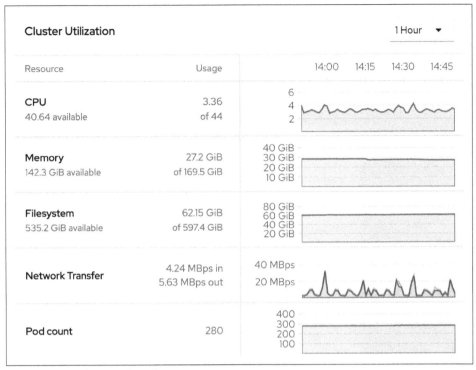

Figure 9-2. Web Console utilization overview

CRC doesn't activate monitoring by default because it requires considerable additional resources beyond CRC's already sizable minimums. This section is intended to give an overview of monitoring facilities, but leaves enabling and experimenting with them mostly as an exercise for the reader.

If you have at least 14 GB of memory available to dedicate to the CRC VM, you can switch on monitoring by stopping, configuring, and restarting CRC:

```
$ crc stop
$ crc config set enable-cluster-monitoring true
$ crc start -m 14336 -c 6
```

Once it's enabled, monitoring cannot be disabled on a given cluster. Instead, you'll need to create a new cluster after setting the enable-cluster-monitoring parameter back to `false`.

Monitoring in the Web Console Developer Perspective

The Monitoring item in the Developer perspective's main navigation includes a ready-made Dashboard of graphs depicting a selected project's consumption of CPU, memory, and other compute resources (Figure 9-3).

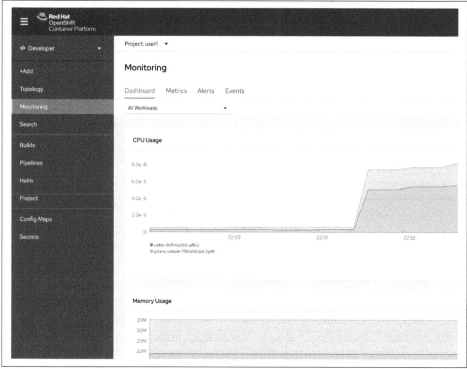

Figure 9-3. Monitoring a Project in the Developer perspective

Monitoring a Deployment

Within a Topology view of a Project, you can check the same basic consumption measurements for just a Deployment or DeploymentConfig. Click on a Deployment in the Topology view to slide its details panel in from the right. The panel's Monitoring tab graphs the resources consumed by the deployment or other component selected in the topology (Figure 9-4).

Figure 9-4. Monitoring a Deployment in a Project topology

Deleting Resources, Applications, and Projects

Once you've built, extended, examined, and managed the exercises in this book, you may want to remove their pieces to reclaim cluster capacity or just to be tidy. The simplest way to do this is to remove the entire project containing those resources. OpenShift will remove the project and all the resources in it:

```
$ oc delete project o4d-hello
project.project.openshift.io "o4d-hello" deleted
```

Sometimes a team or developer is instead granted one project on the cluster, so there might be more than one application and you may need to delete more selectively. You've already used labels to select a subset of resources tagged with an arbitrary key and value. Apply the same technique to first get resources as a test, and then to delete resources matching the label. This time, however, instead of matching labeled resources of a certain kind, you can use the all identifier to get a list of any resource with a matching label:

```
$ oc get all --selector app=noted-app
```

oc will print a list of the matching resources in your current namespace, which is assumed to be the Noted project you created with the exercises in this book. Once you've validated the list of resources with a matching label, pass the same `selector` to the `delete` subcommand:

```
$ oc delete all --selector  app=noted-app
route.project.openshift.io "noted" deleted
...
```

Summary

This chapter highlighted commands and Web Console controls for managing, monitoring, and troubleshooting applications. It also showed how resource consumption and activity are graphed at the cluster, project, and deployment levels in the OpenShift Web Console. You have the basic skills you need to manage your applications on OpenShift, and also to look for clues when things go wrong.

In Chapter 10, you'll learn more about automating some of the rote labor of deploying and managing applications with OpenShift Templates and Kubernetes Operators. You've already used Operators to manage the database for your Noted application. Operators automatically manage services you depend on, and you can create Operators to package your application as a managed deployment for your customers.

Templates, Operators, and OpenShift Automation

You've used templates and Operators throughout this book. Both automate repetitive tasks. This chapter provides more detail about these two mechanisms and relates them to the principle of automation in OpenShift. Triggering builds and deployments when source code changes, restarting failed pods, and an Operator upgrading your application's database server are all ways of delegating to software some of the toil of operating software.

An OpenShift template automates the creation of a set of resources so that it can describe, for example, an application's components and then be repeatedly processed to deploy that application. An Operator also deploys an application and its resources, but an Operator continues to watch and govern those resources over their entire life cycle. The most advanced Operators turn their applications into managed services. You took steps in an administrator role to set up Operators for Pipelines and other services. But consider the process after that was done: back in your developer role, you selected and instantiated services in your Project without much concern for the details of their deployment and administration. The Operator created the resources, started the services, and kept them running so that you could use them in your application.

Templates

A template is a list of objects and the named parameters of their configuration. Each time OpenShift processes a template, it inserts values for the template's parameters from command-line arguments or Web Console forms. Special values can signal the template processor to populate those parameters with random strings or other input it generates. Template metadata can inform the processor of criteria for validating proposed values.

A template can define a set of labels to apply to every object in the template. For example, services, build configurations, and deployments can be defined in templates and then repeatedly created even in a shared Project namespace by processing the template with a set of appropriate variables.

Templates in the OpenShift Web Console

You used a template in Chapter 4's Hello World application, and again in Chapter 6 to create the ngrok proxy that relays GitHub webhooks to your CRC cluster. The Go language builder you used in Chapter 4 is defined as a template with an annotation that identifies it as a "builder" and a parameter specifying a Git repository with the source to be built. To check out other templates, click Add from the Developer perspective. When presented with the Developer Catalog, check the Template box to filter the listing to just those catalog items defined in a template, as shown in Figure 10-1.

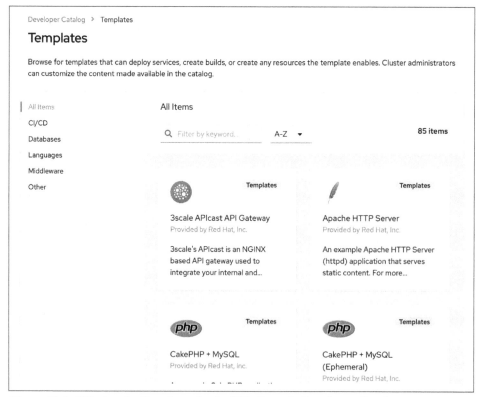

Figure 10-1. Filtering for Templates in the Web Console Developer Catalog

Inspecting templates

You can also list a cluster's templates with the API get verb, like any other cluster resource. OpenShift Templates included with a particular cluster install are in the openshift Project namespace, so direct oc get to look there with the -n openshift argument:

```
$ oc get templates -n openshift
NAME                      DESCRIPTION
[...]
Nginx-example             An example Nginx HTTP server and a reverse...
Nodejs-mongodb-example    An example Node.js application with a Mong...
Openjdk-web-basic-s2i     An example Java application using OpenJDK....
[...]
```

Processing templates with oc process

You can list and create the objects from a template with the command-line oc tool. If a template has been uploaded to your cluster, you can refer to it by its namespace and name. oc can also process a template in a YAML file that has not been added to the cluster by specifying the file path with oc process -f file.yaml.

The oc process subcommand processes a template, combining it with provided parameters to produce a YAML manifest for the template objects on the standard output. You can run process and check the output. Once it's correct, run process again, piping the output to oc create to actually create the objects.

In the following shell excerpts, the nginx-example template's objects are examined, then piped to oc create:

```
$ oc process -n openshift nginx-example
{
      "kind": "List",
      "apiVersion": "v1",
      "metadata": {},
      "items": [
  {
      "apiVersion": "v1",
      "kind": "Service",
      "metadata": {
          "annotations": {
              "description": "Exposes and load balances the application pods"
          },
          "labels": {
              "template": "nginx-example"
          },
          "name": "nginx-example"
      },
      "spec": {
[...]
```

`oc` `process` will list all the template's configurable parameters, in case you need to adjust any of the defaults after inspecting the output:

```
$ oc process --parameters -n openshift nginx-example
NAME                    The name assigned to all of the frontend
nginx-example              objects defined in this template.

NAMESPACE               The OpenShift Namespace where the ImageStream
openshift                  Resides.

NGINX_VERSION           Version of NGINX image to be used (1.16-el8 by
1.16-el8                   default).

MEMORY_LIMIT            Maximum amount of memory the container can use.
512Mi
```

You can set these parameters on the `oc` `process` command line with successive `-p` or `--param` arguments giving the parameter and value to set. In the following example, the template's default `NAME` parameter is changed from `nginx-example` to `nginx-two`.

Notice the trailing dash ("-") in the invocation of `oc` `create` `-f` `-`. It indicates that `oc` should read from the standard input:

```
$ oc process -n openshift nginx-example -p NAME=nginx-two | oc create -f -
service/nginx-two created
route.route.openshift.io/nginx-two created
imagestream.image.openshift.io/nginx-two created
buildconfig.build.openshift.io/nginx-two created
deploymentconfig.apps.openshift.io/nginx-two created
```

After piping the template objects to `oc` `create`, you'll have a simple nginx web server running in your project. You can check with `oc` or see the new nginx deployment in the Web Console Developer Topology view:

```
$ oc get dc nginx-two
NAME        REVISION  DESIRED  CURRENT  TRIGGERED BY
Nginx-two 1           1        1        config,image(nginx-two:latest)
```

Creating Your Own Templates

You can define new templates to control the creation and repeated deployment of your own applications. The template defines the objects it creates along with some metadata to guide the creation of those objects.

The following is an example of a template object definition. As you can see, templates are defined in YAML manifests like other resources:

```
apiVersion: v1
kind: Template
metadata:
  name: redis-template
```

```
    annotations:
      description: "Description"
      iconClass: "icon-redis"
      tags: "database,nosql"
  objects:
    - apiVersion: v1
      kind: Pod
      metadata:
        name: redis-master
      spec:
        containers:
          - env:
            - name: REDIS_PASSWORD
              value: ${REDIS_PASSWORD}
            image: dockerfile/redis
            name: master
            ports:
              - containerPort: 6379
                protocol: TCP
  parameters:
  - description: Password used for Redis authentication
    from: '[A-Z0-9]{8}'
    generate: expression
    name: REDIS_PASSWORD
  labels:
    redis: master
```

The all-caps keywords are the parameters for properties that should vary each time the objects in the template are created. Notice that this template designates the REDIS_PASSWORD as a generated parameter and sets the range of characters from which it should be generated. For more on creating templates, see the OpenShift documentation (*https://oreil.ly/IAppK*).

Operators

An Operator knows how to deploy its application's resources. But unlike a template, an Operator keeps running and it knows how to keep its application running. Operators manage applications with persistent state, or with their own notion of clustering, where failure recovery or scaling requires more than just restarting interchangeable replicas. Operator authors create custom controller code that understands a specific application's internal state and can, for instance, issue credentials, reconnect persistent storage, or arrange a node hierarchy as in a database cluster where some members are write leaders and others are followers.

Operators adopt the key Kubernetes concept, the reconcile loop, watching application-specific custom resources to continuously shepherd them toward a desired state. They adopt Kubernetes API conventions. They can build atop and use native Kubernetes resources. They can be addressed and manipulated with the usual tools like any other Kubernetes object.

Operator Subscriptions and the Operator Lifecycle Manager

You dealt with Operators from beginning to end when you installed the Pipelines Operator in Chapter 5, and to provide a database for your application in Chapter 7. As a cluster admin, you used the Administrator perspective's OperatorHub to add a subscription for each Operator.

A subscription declares that an Operator should be installed on the cluster, and sets parameters for how the Operator should be updated and in which Projects or namespaces it should be available. As an Operator manages installation and upgrades for its application, a cluster component called the Operator Lifecycle Manager (OLM) acts as an Operator for Operators, managing the installation and life cycle of Operators on a cluster in accordance with the cluster's subscriptions. Details of OLM and Operator subscriptions are beyond the scope of this book, but you can learn more about Operator internals, OLM subscriptions, and how to build Operators at the OpenShift Operators page and in *Kubernetes Operators* by Jason Dobies and Joshua Wood (O'Reilly).

Operators from the Developer Perspective

In many production OpenShift Deployments, developers will use Operator-backed services like any other catalog item, without making cluster-wide decisions about which Operators are installed. Administrators subscribe to an appropriate set of Operators. Developers consume the applications those Operators manage from the Developer Catalog.

Operators shepherd foundation services with custom logic and make adding a database, a message queue, or other common components similar to using a managed cloud service. The Operator pattern lets you construct Kubernetes native applications that not only run on Kubernetes platforms like OpenShift, but also make use of platform resources, obey platform conventions, and apply platform automation principles.

Summary

This chapter investigated Operators and templates to illustrate the principle of automation in OpenShift. In earlier chapters, you learned how to deploy and incrementally improve an application on the platform. You used OpenShift Pipelines to automate your application's release process, watching OpenShift build and run your app with cluster horsepower each time you committed changes to its source code. You used OpenShift features like the Developer Catalog and Operators to quickly deploy managed services. You've practiced daily application care and grooming on OpenShift, and have an idea of where to look when things go wrong.

When things go right, you can focus on improving your applications. OpenShift builds the latest release, rolls it out, scales it, and keeps it running until your next killer feature or bug fix triggers the cycle again.

Index

About the Authors

Joshua Wood is a principal developer advocate at Red Hat. Joshua was formerly responsible for documentation at CoreOS and coauthored *Kubernetes Operators* (O'Reilly). Wood has worked in roles from sysadmin to CTO to build utility computing with open source software. He likes fast cars, slow boats, and writing short autobiographies.

Brian Tannous is a principal developer advocate at Red Hat. He is a founder at GT Media where he builds mobile applications. Throughout his career, Brian has held development, marketing, and advocacy roles in distributed computing, mobile, and open source technology.

Colophon

The bird on the cover of *OpenShift for Developers* is a black-headed caique (*Pionites melanocephalus*), also known as the black-headed or black-capped parrot. They inhabit mostly humid forest areas in the Amazon (north of the Amazon River), Brazil (to the west of the Ucayali River), northern Bolivia, Colombia, Ecuador, French Guiana, Guyana, Peru, Suriname, and Venezuela.

The black-headed caique has a short tail, black crown, yellow-orangeish head, white belly, yellow thighs, and green wings, back, and upper tail. Males and females have identical plumage; the only way to distinguish them is through surgical sexing or DNA sexing. Wild caiques often have a brownish stained breast; their captive cousins have white there instead. They are popular among parrot breeders and keepers.

Black-headed caiques are often found in pairs or small flocks of up to 10 to 30 birds. They mostly eat flowers, pulp, seeds, and possibly insects. The birds use their beaks more than other parrot species and tend to bite. They mimic sounds such as alarms, smoke detectors, microwave beeps, laughs, and whistles. Caiques also combine sounds in their vocabulary to form new sounds.

Many of the animals on O'Reilly covers are endangered; all of them are important to the world.

The color illustration is by Karen Montgomery, based on a black and white engraving from *Heck's Nature and Science*. The cover fonts are Gilroy Semibold and Guardian Sans. The text font is Adobe Minion Pro; the heading font is Adobe Myriad Condensed; and the code font is Dalton Maag's Ubuntu Mono.

O'REILLY®

There's much more where this came from.

Experience books, videos, live online training courses, and more from O'Reilly and our 200+ partners—all in one place.

Learn more at oreilly.com/online-learning

Milton Keynes UK
Ingram Content Group UK Ltd.
UKHW010657060924
447889UK00016B/127